Life in the Mouse House

Life in the Mouse House
MEMOIR OF A DISNEY STORY ARTIST

Homer Brightman

Theme Park Press

© 2014 Pamela Etzler and Connie Heller-Zeiger

All rights reserved. Printed in the United States of America. Except as permitted under the United States Copyright Act of 1976, no part of this publication may be reproduced or distributed in any form or by any means, or stored in a database or retrieval system, without prior written permission of the publisher.

This book is not authorized, sponsored, or endorsed by The Walt Disney Company or by any of its subsidiaries. It is an unofficial and unauthorized book and not a Disney product.

The mention of names and places associated with The Walt Disney Company is used in context for educational purposes and is not meant to infringe on any existing Disney copyrights or registered Disney trademarks.

The author is not affiliated with, nor is he a representative of, The Walt Disney Company. The opinions and statements expressed in this book are solely those of the author and/or the people quoted by the author and do not necessarily reflect the opinions and policies of The Walt Disney Company or Theme Park Press.

While every precaution has been taken in the preparation of this book, neither the author nor Theme Park Press assume responsibility for errors or omissions. Neither is any liability assumed for damages resulting, or alleged to result, directly or indirectly from the use of the information contained herein.

Editor: Bob McLain
Layout: Artisanal Text
Cover Design: Emily White

First Printing, 2014
ISBN 978-0-9843415-2-8

Theme Park Press | www.ThemeParkPress.com
Address queries to bob@themeparkpress.com

If you have a Disney or pop culture story to tell, Theme Park Press would like to help you tell it. We offer generous compensation and the most author-friendly terms in the business. See how we can put you in print:

www.ThemeParkPress.com/write-for-us

Names have been changed but the facts are true.

"The time has come," the Walrus said,
"To talk of many things:
Of shoes—and ships—and sealing wax
Of cabbages—and Kings—
And why the sea is boiling hot—
And whether pigs have wings."

—Lewis Carroll

Contents

Foreword xi

Preface xv

Editor's Introduction xix

Introduction xxiii

Chapter One 1

Chapter Two 11

Chapter Three 21

Chapter Four 27

Chapter Five 31

Chapter Six 41

Chapter Seven 45

Chapter Eight 55

Chapter Nine 61

Chapter Ten 67

Chapter Eleven 71

Chapter Twelve 83

Chapter Thirteen 87

Chapter Fourteen 91

Homer Brightman: Life After Disney 95

Homer Brightman:
Filmography and Comicography 101

Notes 115

About the Author 119

About the Editor 121

About the Publisher 123

Index 125

More Books from Theme Park Press 129

Foreword

I grew up hearing stories. After all, my grandfather, Homer, was a storyteller, both by nature and by vocation. He told me stories, laughing, about the pranks he pulled on his two daughters: my mother, Connie, and her younger sister, my aunt Pam. There were simple things, such as replacing their regular breakfast milk with pure buttermilk, and more complex tricks, like when he put an inflation device under my mother's dinner plate and each time she would start to take a bite, her plate would rise! He loved gags!

There were only two things my grandfather loved more than a good gag; one of those was the sea. Sailing was his first love and his lifelong love. He was born October 1, 1901, in Port Townsend, Washington, on the edge of the Pacific coast. His father, Homer H. Swaney, the president of Seattle Iron and Steel Company, died in those rough waters when my father was two years old, the result of a tragic ferry boat accident. As an adult, Grandpa Homer decorated his house with pictures of magnificent sailing ships on stormy seas, water crashing over the decks. We would stand together and talk about those paintings.

"Was it really like this, out there?" I would ask, finding it hard to believe, sure there was exaggeration on the canvas.

"That's the way she was," he would reply, telling stories of the sea from his Merchant Marine days.

He told me the story of how he ran away from home at fifteen to join the Merchant Marines[1]. He loved sailing to the Orient and spoke highly of the skilled dentist in Shanghai who put the gold between his teeth. Over and over, I heard how his life was saved on one trip to China by a giant sea turtle. A huge wave took him overboard, when he was the third mate and the night watchman. He was just about to give up—three hours in the cold water—not able to tread water one minute longer, when out of the churning sea came this giant turtle. He was able to hold onto it until the boat came back for him.

My favorite story, however, was the very short story of his birth. Every one of us heard this story whenever we asked him where he was born. Port Townsend never once came out of his mouth.

"I was not born. I had no parents. I was found strapped to a log, floating in the sea."

We were never quite sure if that was the truth, so we all kept asking! I was, however, sure about the sea turtle story, and I never tired of hearing it. Growing up, I often thought my own life would not have been, had this turtle not saved him!

He was so convincing when he spoke! He acted out every story, throwing his arms in the air like waves, flapping his hands like wings, as he told me the story of the waterlogged bee he saved, flying directly at him and putting him in the pool fully dressed.

There are many references in the volumes of Disney biographies to Homer Brightman being quite demonstrative in the telling of his stories, during his days working at the Disney Studio as a storyboard artist. One recounts his telling of a Donald Duck cartoon and the entire room going to pieces in laughter. Walt turns to his stenographer and asks her if she is laughing at the story, to which she replies, "At Homer!"

If tuberculosis had not gotten hold of my grandfather in the 1920s, he might have stayed sailing the seas his entire life. A doctor landlocked him in a sanatorium in Chicago. A few months later he sent away for a basic drawing course. He recovered and began sending cartoons to the *Saturday Evening Post*. As you will read, he made his way to the Disney Studios in the 1930s, where he worked for free the first few weeks and then for $15 a week.

It is there, in southern California, where he brought stories to life for Walt Disney, and settled into his own life with the other thing he loved more than gags: his family. He and my grandmother, Rosalind Smith Brightman, raised my mom and my aunt on Lee Drive. Homer became a member of a small group of men who were known as the Disney storyboard artists. This is where he reinvented fairy tales and gave his characters a voice. He told me in his later years his favorite creation, favorite character of all, was the shy, plump mouse, Octavius, known as "Gus Gus", from the movie *Cinderella*. He wrote all the mice into the story, giving them personalities and bringing them to life.

When I watch his movies or cartoons I feel I am once again sitting beside him, listening to his stories and laughing. His personal characteristics of kindness, generosity, and his original sense of humor shine through in his work. It is in the movie *Mickey and the Beanstalk*, in particular, that I recognize him. My grandfather's personality is there in Donald, Goofy, and Mickey as they sit at the kitchen table, slicing the bread and the very last bean!

In my family, one also heard stories of that famous man on the television, Walt Disney. My grandfather clearly loved his work, but not working for Walt. There is always more than one side to a story, and, as we learned, more than one side to Walt Disney. Yes, he was the smiling man on the television Sunday evenings. However, I heard stories of how he behaved toward his employees, never giving them credit, grumbling as he walked down the hallways smoking a cigarette, or scowling at them when he bumped into them in the restrooms at the Studio. Walt was the kind face and warm voice I enjoyed on TV, but Grandpa Homer described a very serious, driven, and unfriendly man, off-screen. Life in the "Mouse House", as my grandfather called it, could often be unpleasant and stressful. Good thing my grandpa Homer always kept his sense of humor.

My grandfather lives on in time, through his stories and characters, through his children and grandchildren. The Disney Studio grew over time and became a large company with a life of its own; however, when you return to its foundation, go back to the Golden Age of Disney, you will find Homer Brightman and a group of hard-working, talented "gag-men" who came together and gave the world the gift of their stories.

Melinda Heller Nellos
January 2014

Preface

High on a shelf, in a dusty old box, alone in a closet, sat a story waiting to be told for over thirty years. The story contained our father's experiences over a fifteen-year period when he was employed at what he loved to call the Fantasy Factory—the Disney Studio. It was not until this spring, when Didier Ghez, a long-time Disney enthusiast and historian, tracked my sister and I down, in search of one more hidden memoir of the long-lost artists that were in the employ of Walt Disney during those wonderful Golden Years of the 1930s, that the book came out of the box.

In January 1904, en route to Victoria, British Columbia, for business, Homer's father, Homer Swaney, was aboard the steamship *Clallam*, carrying over ninety passengers. During the night, the *Clallam* encountered hurricane-force winds, leaving her adrift until she finally sank in the Straits of Juan de Fuca, only miles from Victoria. Mildred, left with two small sons to raise (Homer had one younger brother John who was born in 1903), moved to Seattle, Washington. Years later, she married Frank Brightman, adding two daughters to the now lively family of four. Our father always had dreams as a young boy, now living on Mercer Island, of being a sea captain sailing the world. He would take his mother each week across Lake Washington on the family skiff to Steward Park to catch a horse-drawn buggy that would carry them to the Pike Street Market for their weekly shopping. He often told of how he would see himself in that skiff, sailing the seas with heroic stories of pirates, adventure, and far-away lands. At the age of seventeen, he attended a Maritime Academy in Seattle, where he received certification in high seas navigation and a second-mate license.

After completion of his studies, he was employed by the Robert Dollar Steamship Lines, based in Seattle, working as an apprentice on sailing ships. Then, in 1919, he boarded the *A.V. Gregory*, bound for Sydney, Australia. Often we would listen to the heroic and scary stories of the crew as they sailed around Cape Horn in wintry conditions. Later in his career he was raised to the position of second mate, sailing on large freighters across the Pacific to the Orient. Dad was soon offered a position in the Shanghai offices for two years, and then transferred to Hong Kong and later to Singapore, where he was under employ for eight years.

Upon returning to New York on business for the Dollar Steamship Lines, he met up with his folks for a much-needed visit. It was at that time his family saw that he was not well and scheduled him to see their family doctor. Our dad received the diagnosis of an advance case of tuberculosis and was given six months to live. Needless to say, he had staying power. It was during those many years of recovery that he would formulate stories of his travels to the delight of many of the patients that were working toward recovery themselves.

After three years of convalescence in a sanatorium in Tucson, Arizona, he was discharged and traveled back to Chicago to be with his family. It was there that he met our mother, who had recently graduated from Beloit College in Wisconsin and was working as a fill-in secretary for our grandfather. He adored our mother, and they were married on July 24th, 1935, in Chicago. They had a long, wonderful forty years of marriage, leaving both my sister and I with incredible role models. Our dad would often say, years after mom's death, that he would never marry again, since "When life gives you the best friend and wife ever, why would you want for more?"

Every Sunday was our day: girls' day out with Dad! We loved it! Often, he would take us to Griffith Park to ride on the carousel, for what seemed hours at a time. We would then go to the zoo to make it a day, and sometimes stop by downtown Glendale on the way home for hot-fudge Sundays, or, better yet, stop by this tiny little take-out stand, run by a local school teacher, for sliced barbecue beef and ribs. He claimed it was the best barbecue he had ever eaten in his life, and I have to agree—it was special.

Dad loved to swim, and had a swimming pool built in our backyard. When he came home from work, he would always make a grand entrance with a huge splash and play with our friends, tossing us in the air, and always turning time in the pool with giant races; races, of course, that he never won.

He always loved animals and our home, at times, seemed to have just too many pets. We had a cat named Tuffy; a dog, whom we adored, named Billie; and every Easter we each would get a pink and blue baby chick, much to our mother's chagrin. We also had two miniature turtles that lived in a bowl with plastic palm trees that sometimes found their way out of their cramped surroundings, and it was always a task locating them. One day they just disappeared, never to return, and I always felt Mom had something to do with that.

Our father was always a born storyteller, even from a young age, and both my sister and I would sit with the fondest memories of our time spent with him as he would go over his storyboard drawings like he was handling a deck of cards. Often, he would stop and say, "Why didn't you laugh?", and when we would explain he would drop that gag and go back to the drawing board. He always wanted to make us laugh, and he was never short of jokes and fun antics.

Our parents loved to dance, and both my sister and I loved nothing more than going to the Oakmont Country Club for dinner and getting to dance with Dad. They had this very tiny, little organ that an older lady would play for hours. We loved watching Mom and Dad dance while waiting our special turn with Dad. Those were memorable times, when we could feel all grown-up, waltzing around the dance floor with Dad all to ourselves. Dad was devoted to his family, but our time with him did come with a hidden cost. My bedroom was close to the kitchen and often, when I would get up in the middle of the night, Dad would be sitting, hunched over his drawing board, at our kitchen table, coming up with a story and gags to make children laugh. He spent a great deal of time working at two and three in the morning, yet always seemed full of pep the next day, coffee in hand, talking with Mom while she prepared breakfast for us before heading out to school. It wasn't until later in life, when both my sister and I became parents ourselves, that we did marvel at what a kid at heart our father was, and how and where he always found the time for us, be it combing the beach at Balboa for shells, teaching us to jump rope, ride bicycles, climb trees. It was his wonderful way of showing us his love.

Dad never tired of telling stories and making people laugh, and in his later years, while living in a retirement home, he would help others who were less fortunate than himself. Several such men who sat at his table for meals were stroke victims and had lost the use of their voices. It made ordering a meal laborious and hard for them, so at each meal Dad would bring to the table his old grease pencils and draw pictures of each menu item on the paper tablecloths, along with the condiments and salad dressings, so they could point to the item of choice. Of course, the items he drew sometimes did not make the food look delicious, depending on what Dad liked or disliked, so it was not uncommon to see our father in serious discussion with the head chef, much to the delight of his silent friends. They loved him, as he made their disability a little more tolerable, adding humor to their struggles.

Pamela Etzler and Connie Heller-Zeiger
January 2014

Editor's Introduction

Most of the talented artists who knew and worked with Walt Disney are gone. Those who have never or seldom been interviewed took their precious memories to the grave.

Or did they?

Thankfully, for Disney history addicts like myself, there are still hidden autobiographies and memoirs to be unearthed: from the legendary 1938–1948 diaries of animator Ward Kimball; to the not-yet-released autobiography of concept artist Mel Shaw, *Animator of Horseback*; or the recently discovered notes of Eric Larson for his book *50 Years in the Mouse House*. Needless to say, those documents are extremely rare and of uppermost value to Disney historians and Disney enthusiasts alike. So when I found traces of a memoir written by a story artist of Disney's Golden Age, in the archives of Disney historian Michael Barrier, I knew that I had hit "pay dirt". The story artists worked closer to Walt than any of the other artists, and they were at the center of the Studio's creative process. The '30s were the most exciting creative period at the Studio. And Homer Brightman, despite having collaborated on dozens of shorts and quite a few features, was one of the lesser-known artists of that era. I knew that his book would be fascinating and enlightening.

After tracking down Homer's daughters, Pamela Etzler and Connie Heller-Zeiger, and after reading the book, I was glad to confirm that its contents are indeed exhilarating from a Disney history standpoint.

There are dozens and dozens of stories in this volume which are either brand new or shed new light on what we already knew: hilarious memories of fellow story artists Harry Reeves, Perce Pearce, Roy Williams, Webb Smith, and many others; new information about the career of animator Frenchy de Trémaudan; new details about the events of the 1941 Studio strike; and, almost on every page, new elements that help us "connect the dots" when it comes to artists and events. In other words, I learned something exciting and fun in each chapter.

But there is also a darker side to Homer Brightman's memoir. One can feel that his fifteen years at the Studio were not a happy time professionally and emotionally. The man we discover is one who, while at the Disney Studio, suffered due to internal politics, constant fear of losing his job, and artistic frustrations. This unhappiness leads to a very dark portrait of Walt. We all know that Walt was not a saint and could be a harsh taskmaster. Many of Homer's colleagues, however, had a very different point of view on Walt as a boss and as a human being. Many of those positive perspectives are shared in the pages of the book series *Walt's People*.

In other words, as is always the case when reading an autobiography, it is important to keep in mind that Homer Brightman's perspective is subjective. His point of view is nonetheless a very important one, his story fascinating, and his prose so clear that his book, from day one, is a delight to read.

When he completed his book in 1986, Homer decided to hide the names of his co-workers behind pseudonyms. Homer's daughters, Pam and Connie, felt that the body of the book had to be released exactly as Homer had left it, with the only addition of a few endnotes to clarify a few facts and the rare faulty memories. Thankfully, both also realized that the book takes another dimension when one knows who are the artists hidden behind the pseudonyms. I am therefore enclosing below a list of the names of the individuals we believe we identified, thanks to notes left by Brightman as well as some additional research completed while working on this manuscript. I strongly encourage you to make reference to this list while reading Homer's memoir.

Life in the Mouse House is an enlightening adventure, which for Homer ironically started on a grey morning of February 1935...

Didier Ghez
Coral Gables
December 2013

The "Cast"

Animation Director = Jack Kinney

Apalini = Bianca Majolie

Argentine Artist = F. Molina Campos

Barker = Pinto Colving

Belter = Jack Hannah

Bigger = Frank Tashlin

Boney Australian = Ken O'Connor

Chief Agitator = Art Babbitt

Chilby = Eddie Strickland

Clem Longshanks = Carl Barks

Crock = Card Walker

Diddle = Joe Grant

Dill = Ernie Terrazas

Dodger = Norman Ferguson

Dogstone = George Drake

Duddleham = Otto Englander

Fluk = Probably Carl Fallberg

Former Polo Player = James Bodrero

Gabbey = Tom Wood

Gloomy Gus = Ted Thwaites

Grout = Dick Lundy

Henry = Unidentified

Hispanic Animator = Rudy Zamora

Hogsworth = Roy Scott

Ivy Green = Mary Flanigan

Jiggins = Earl Hurd

Kinch = Ben Sharpsteen

Kipper = Wilfred Jackson

Links = Ham Luske

Loganbary = Josh Meador

MacPew = McLaren Stewart

Mert Kibble = Joe Grant

Monks = Frenchy de Trémaudan

Muggle = Ken Anderson

Number Two = Dave Hand

Pophoff = Harry Reeves

Sligh = Ted Sears

Smirks = Harry Tytle

Snojob = Perce Pearce

Stiltwalker = Bill Roberts

Strayshott = Webb Smith

Suggs = Roy Williams

Titcomb = Jack Miller

Tricklebank = Frank Teague

Wetmore = Hal Adelquist

Zaire = Mary Blair

Introduction

Walt Disney was, in the eyes of millions, one of the truly outstanding Americans. He brought joy and happiness to the world, laughter to the multitudes, and clean, wholesome family entertainment to people everywhere. He was a modern-day Pied Piper; and, like the fluter of Hamlin town, he was a man with a mission. He knew where he wanted to go and how to get there.

When he died in 1966, he had won thirty-two Academy Awards; five Emmys; honorary degrees from Harvard, Yale, USC, and UCLA; and, among others, the Presidential Medal of Freedom. His path through life was studded with glories.

Walt won accolades from his peers, and he also toted up an impressive list of physical assets. At his death, the corporation he controlled was worth over $100,000,000, including subsidiary companies for domestic film distribution; a phonograph record division and a music company; WED Enterprises[2], which designs rides for Disneyland; and WED's subsidiary, MAPO, which engineers the rides that WED designs. Walt Disney Productions owned a 51-acre studio in Burbank, 100 acres of Disneyland at Anaheim, additional buildings in Glendale (all in California), and property twice the size of Manhattan near Orlando, Florida, site of Walt Disney World. In addition, there was his private company, Retlaw (Walter spelled backward), which reputedly owns and manages apartment houses, ranch land, radio and television stations, and assorted incomeproducing enterprises.

All this, and Walt had started from a broken-down garage in Los Angeles.

Chapter One

As I read about Walt Disney and hear about the many facets of his genius—even now many years after his death—I remember what I experienced.

Walt wasn't in his "broken-down garage" when I first arrived in Hollywood, but the facilities were far from luxurious. My first glimpse of the Disney Studio on that gray morning in early February 1935 was a big letdown. I had dreamed of bright California sunshine, bluebirds whistling among the lilacs, and a studio nestling in the hollow of cozy green hills, like one of his charming Silly Symphonies. There were the hills, but they were a moth-eaten brown and studded with box-shaped stucco houses.

I walked down Hyperion Avenue east of Hollywood, past steep vacant lots spewing their crumbling banks onto the sidewalks. I came to the intersection of Griffith Park Boulevard, and across the street was a Shell gas station. Behind it, half hidden in back of a weathered wall, was a red tile roof. The wall ended in a rambling Spanish-type hacienda at 2719 Hyperion Avenue. A sign hanging above the door announced: WALT DISNEY PRODUCTIONS LTD.

I shoved the door. It stuck. I shoved again. The door gave, and I stumbled into a gloomy little reception room with carved Spanish-type wooden bars screening the window. A switchboard operator gave me an indifferent glance and slipped off her earphones. I said I had an appointment with Mr. Stiltwalker, an animator. She plugged in a line, and, after a couple of minutes, said, "Somebody out here to see you, Sam. Okay?" Wordlessly, she pointed to another door leading to a larger building. I crossed a patch of brown grass and saw that it was two stories high with a little grillwork balcony on the second floor overlooking the lawn.

Inside the main building, the welcome aroma of hot coffee filled the air. The delightful odor wafted from a spot to the left of the stairs, where there was a cubbyhole, its shelves heaped with cartons of cigarettes and candy bars. The doors which enclosed it were wide open, and on their inside panels hung a rack of pipes, a lopsided calendar, and an Old Gold cigarette ad. The little counter was littered with coffee cups, overflowing ashtrays, and a box half-filled with assorted doughnuts. I was to learn later that doughnuts were Walt's favorite breakfast food.

A chubby little brunette was in charge of the shop. She smiled and asked, "Coffee?"

I shook my head. "Where can I find Mr. Stiltwalker?"

She obligingly ducked under the counter and beckoned for me to follow her. As we walked down a long hall with doors opening off it, we introduced ourselves. "I'm Ivy Green," she said, looking back over her shoulder, "and I run the store. Coffee's a nickel a cup. You can get it any time you want it, but don't hang around. Walt doesn't like the fellows to hang around and gab. He says it takes away from production."

She stopped and opened a door. "Someone to see you, Sam."

A short, wiry man in a tattered gray sweater swung around from his drawing board, got up, and shook hands. I handed him a letter of introduction from a mutual cartoonist friend in Chicago. Stiltwalker read the letter and tacked it to his drawing board with a push pin.

"How's Henry?" His voice had a nasal twang.

"Fine. He said to give you his regards."

"Nice fellow." Stiltwalker held out a workman's hand, red and rough. "Got your samples?"

I passed him my book of clippings containing cartoons published in various magazines. He leafed through them without expression while I thought, "Jesus, this guy is the personification of enthusiasm."

Still looking at the drawings he said, "I don't think you'll make an animator. You don't draw like one."

My knees buckled. I had set my heart on getting a job at Disney's. I told him I was sure I could make the grade. All I asked for was a chance.

I didn't tell him I had already written to Walt Disney from Chicago asking for a tryout. I didn't know, but, at the time, Walt and his brother Roy were in Europe.[3] My samples were returned by Walt's private secretary, with a discouraging letter dated January 22, 1935, in which she said, "No one who is not permanently situated near Los

Angeles can be considered as an applicant." She finished by saying, "We absolutely and definitely ask you not to come to California on the strength of getting a position in this studio." (I came to California anyway and here I was.)

"I would appreciate the opportunity to prove myself, Mr. Stiltwalker," I said. "After all, I've come a long way."

He agreed, and, picking up the phone, said, "I'll call Dogstone. He's head of the Inbetween Department and handles all animation tryouts." He got Dogstone on the phone. "Doug, I've got a friend of mine out here from Chicago. Give him a tryout, will you?"

He listened for a moment and then said, "Nine o'clock tomorrow? Thanks, Doug."

I walked out of the studio on air and hardly realized I had boarded a red Hollywood Boulevard streetcar and had gotten off at Western. I was clear down on Sunset rounding the corner to my boarding house before I came to.

That night my unheated room was colder than an iceman's hand, but I spread my overcoat over the cheap blanket and didn't move until my alarm went off next morning. I got up early, shaved in cold water, went to the corner drug store, and ate a breakfast of cold ham and eggs. I thought everybody in California was nuts; they left their doors open. What were they trying to prove—that California was hot? I had just come from Chicago where snow blew across the Dearborn Street Station, and it was warmer there.

I took the Hollywood Red Car again and got off at the junction, rode a yellow bus to the studio, and reported to Dogstone at nine, sharp. He looked like he should be on a roof hammering nails. His little office had a large glass window covering one wall so that he could keep an eye on the fifteen or twenty inbetweeners already hard at work. He flicked a switch on his desk. "I can hear 'em, too," he said. Then, into a little speaker, "Lay off all that talk, you guys. We're behind schedule." Then he flicked the key to "off" and explained that all applicants were given a two-week tryout at their own expense.

I followed him into a large room without windows and dark as a cave. Dim lights glowed on several desks, where shadowy figures were hard at work. Each man had a desk with a drawing board on it. The board was tilted up at an angle, and in the center was a square of transparent glass through which a light shone. Dogstone said, "Meet another one, fellows."

One or two silhouettes got up and shook hands with me, but most of them labored on. It didn't make any difference; I couldn't have remembered their names anyway. I was too worried about what I was expected to draw. Dogstone left and a young artist named Chilby came in and introduced me to the mysteries of inbetweening. My problem was to make a series of inbetween drawings of the Three Little Pigs dancing. Between the two extremes, I had to make a drawing that would continue the smooth action. The pigs were complete strangers to me, and I spent the whole day trying to get their likenesses.

I was used to noodling out a finished drawing to illustrate my gag line. Inbetweening was something different. An inbetweener had to have a flowing line, work fast, and lay in a smooth transition between drawings. The animator made the extremes, and his assistant added key drawings. The inbetweener did the dirty work of filling in all the drawings needed to keep the scene from jittering. I knew I wouldn't like animation.

Just before lunch, Dogstone looked in on us. A pudgy, middle-aged artist jumped up and matched quarters with him.

The coins spun in the air, and the artist made a great show of uncovering his coin.

"Damn it, I lost again. You win another carton of cigarettes," he cried, yanking open his desk and handing Dogstone a carton of Old Golds.

"I'm getting lucky, Snojob," said Dogstone, as they left the room together.[4]

"Lucky, my ass," said one of the artists. "That guy will get along. He keeps Dogstone in cigarettes."

"Kiss-ass," remarked a thin guy. (I hadn't learned his name.) "He loses a carton of cigarettes to Dogstone a couple of times a week. Snojob always calls tails."

The thin redheaded fellow said, "The sonofabitch has a two-headed quarter."

Everybody laughed. "That's the way to get ahead around here," he said. The lights were on now, and I was able to see my tryout mates. They seemed to me a shabby lot.

"I don't think I'll make it," said the thin fellow. "After you've worked on these stinking pigs for a week, you're ready to heave up."

I agreed with him but said nothing. A boney Australian, who wore glasses, dug into a sack of lunch and began wolfing down a sandwich. I went over and looked at the cigarette dispenser's board. "He can draw pretty good," I said.

"He won't have to draw," said the thin guy. "He'll go places around here. He's foxy."

We split up then, and I went up the street to the "Shack" for a bowl of soup.

After lunch, the thin guy said, "Let's see your samples." I had a few clippings with me, but my book of them was going around the studio to be evaluated. He was impressed. "You don't belong here. You should be in the Story Department."

"I'd like that better than animation," I said. "How'd you get a chance to try out?"

"Through Mr. Stiltwalker. I got a letter of introduction to him."

"He's a hell of a good animator. Terrific on action. I hear the guy used to be a machinist or something like that."

Dogstone came back then with Snojob. "One o'clock. Get rolling, you guys," he said. "You've got less than two weeks to make good." He snapped off the switch for the big overhead light and left the room plunged into blackness.

About three o'clock an animator named Chilby looked in on me. I was discouraged. "I don't even know how to flip the drawings."

Chilby was a slender, soft-spoken guy, and encouraging. "You'll catch on, all at once," he said, and, standing over my shoulder, corrected my drawing with swift, sure strokes. After he left, I sat for a few moments admiring his drawing, smooth, effortless, perfect! I thought about what Stiltwalker had said. He was right. I would never make an animator. The thought filled me with nervous apprehension, and suddenly I got up and left the room.

In the lavatory, two strangers were lined up, and I stepped up to an adjoining place. The man standing next to me looked like a Spaniard. I'd been in Spain and seen his type before. He turned to the other man and asked him how long he had been at the studio.

"A month."

"How do you like it here?"

"Lousy. For my money this guy Disney stinks."

The Spanish-looking character left abruptly, colliding with a man entering the room. "Sorry, Walt," said the new arrival.

The stranger who had just told Walt that he stunk turned white.

"Christ, was that Walt Disney?" he asked.

"None other," the newcomer said. "He got back from Europe yesterday."

"Me and my big mouth," the fellow said. He left without another word.

"What's eating him?" the newcomer asked.

I told him neither one of us knew we had been standing next to Walt Disney and the third man had unwittingly labeled him a stinker.

The stranger shrugged, "The poor bastard will be gone by tomorrow," he said. But he was wrong. The guy was gone before noon.

Toward the end of my second week, a carefully dressed executive type dropped into the tryout room. My spirits dropped when I saw he was carrying my book of cartoon samples.

"We like your gags," he said, and introduced himself as Mr. Hogsworth. "We're giving you a two-week tryout in the Story Department, at your own expense."

A pleasant shiver ran through me. I knew I could make good on gags, and now I could prove it. Hogsworth ordered me to pick up my things and follow him.

The thin guy had been listening, and as I passed his desk he grinned and made a circle with his thumb and forefinger.

The new room was small, with only one window. Hogsworth introduced me to my new roommates, Tricklebank, Titcomb, and MacPew. When they got up to shake hands, I noticed all of them did a peculiar thing. They covered their drawings with blank sheets of paper. I felt instinctively they were afraid I might steal ideas from them. None of them was inclined to be friendly, and they returned to work while Hogsworth made a phone call for pencils and paper and assigned me to a small table in the corner of the room. Before leaving, he told me to turn all my gags for the week in to him before five o'clock on Friday.

"What will I work on?"

He looked at Titcomb and asked if he had a spare story outline. Titcomb handed him one, and he dropped it on my desk.

"Get to work on this. Draw up any gags you can think of."

In the unpleasant silence following his departure, I read the outline—*Wynken, Blynken and Nod*. Three babies sailed through the sky in a wooden shoe and the Story Department wanted: CUTE GAGS... AVOID GAGS THAT ARE TOO SLAPSTICK IN CHARACTER...CAN YOU SEE ANY CUTE WAY OF HANDLING A THUNDERSTORM? ANY COMEDY BUSINESS BETWEEN THE BABIES AND THE RAINDROPS?

Under SUGGESTIONS was the following: PERSONALITY GAGS FOR THE THREE BABIES ARE MOST IMPORTANT. KEEP IN MIND. WYNKEN IS THE BOLD ONE, BLYNKEN THE 'FRAIDY CAT, AND NOD THE SLEEPYHEAD. DON'T SUBMIT GAGS OUT OF LINE WITH THESE PERSONALITIES.

I went over to Titcomb's desk. He covered his sketches again. "Do they want the stuff sketched rough or cleaned up?" I asked.

"Any old way," he replied, looking me right in the eye so I wouldn't be able to look down and see any sketches he hadn't been able to cover up. He was big, with a baby face and curly brown hair. His sleeves were rolled up over surprisingly brawny arms. Tricklebank and MacPew were intent on their work. I went back to my table feeling as lonesome as a lighthouse keeper on Christmas Eve.

Finally, I broke the silence. "Are you fellows trying out?"

Tricklebank, who wore glasses and looked like a mild school teacher, said, "Nope, we're all on the payroll. Titcomb is in the Character Model Department." He indicated MacPew, tight-lipped, ruddy-faced. "He's in Layout and I'm in Story Sketch." He lapsed into silence, and I went back to work on the three babies, thinking these guys won't take any interest in me until they see if I make the grade. They've probably seen other "tryouts" go through their room. I made up my mind not to be one of the failures.

Each Friday for two weeks, I took my pencil sketches upstairs to Hogsworth's office. He never looked at my gags, but merely dropped them into the deep bottom drawer of his desk and always said, "Keep up the good work."

On the Friday I was to end my two-week tryout period, the old paymaster came around with the paychecks and I watched enviously as they were tucked into wallets. I had been told employees were paid only twice a month, and I worked the rest of the day and Saturday in a state of nerves. Saturday evening I walked along Hollywood Boulevard, looking in shop windows, not feeling I could afford to take in a movie. Finally, I turned onto a side street and went into Carpenter's Sandwich Stand. I drooled over "Chicken in the Straw, served unjointed, without silverware, the natural way...nestled in shoe-string potatoes, with salad, giblet gravy, butter-drenched toast and honey. EVERY BIT A TENDER DELIGHT...60 cents."

Too rich for my pocketbook, and so I settled for "Ice cream, large dish...12 cents." In my mind I kept going over my prospects of employment. I was running short of money, and, to date, I had received no word of encouragement. Suppose I was hired on Monday? I would have to wait another two weeks for a paycheck, and I would have been in Hollywood five weeks by the time any money came in, and my cash was already low. What would I do if I wasn't given a job? I hated to think of that possibility. All day Sunday I pounded the Hollywood pavement, hungry and in a dejected state of mind.

Shortly after nine o'clock on Monday morning, I was called up to Hogsworth's office. This was it!

"They've decided to hire you," he said. "You know the hours. Your salary will be $15 a week."[5]

Trembling, I walked out of his office light-headed. (I hadn't been eating regularly.) I went back to the room feeling faint, but a new man.

"I got on," I said.

"Now the trick is to stay on," MacPew said. I ignored his remark, realizing he was a dour Scot.

Things went on as before. I read outlines of stories and tried to draw up funny gags. Titcomb whistled while he worked, and it annoyed the hell out of me. One day I complained in a nice way. The next day I was moved to a bungalow. It was crowded, too, and presided over by a loud, red-faced character named Gabbey, who drew the monthly Silly Symphony page for *Good Housekeeping* magazine. He rated a private office with a skylight over his desk and always worked with his door wide open so he could express his views on any subject that rattled through his brain.

Titcomb was good news compared to Gabbey. This department had nothing to do with stories, and I learned that artists were able to draw and listen to a radio or talk and their production would not be affected. At Disney's, a storyman was expected to produce fast, and, to do it, he had to concentrate; and a fellow like Gabbey could play hell with his chances of survival. I stuffed cotton in my ears and cursed the day my bad judgment led me to complain about Titcomb's whistling, which had me moved away from Story Department contacts. I appealed to Hogsworth, but he said, "We always move new men around." While he spoke, I cast a glance at the deep double drawer of his desk into which he tossed my weekly gags. It was half full. My heart fell. My work was not being seen, and I left his office rubber-legged with his usual, "Keep up the good work," ringing in my ears.

Rumors were circulating that highly qualified, creative people were clamoring to get on the Disney payroll, and I was getting nowhere. Sligh, the head of the Story Department, after hiring me, never had shown the slightest interest in me. In fact, I had never seen him, and I had an eerie feeling my next move would be outside, and it was cold outside. If you were a new cartoonist in 1935, you were a 50-to-1 shot to land at a free soup kitchen.

I was determined to see Sligh and find out where I stood.

Chapter Two

During his lifetime, Walt was applauded for his music; his animation; his use of color and design; his innovations, both in films and amusement parks; and his willingness to test new ideas. Yet those who knew him best and were closest to him regard Walt as a storyteller.

He was at his best telling a story. He started with simple vignettes in *Alice in Cartoonland*, and then his stories became a trifle more complex in the early Mickey and Donald short subjects. His never-to-be-forgotten features, *Snow White and the Seven Dwarfs* and *Cinderella*, were storytelling at its best. Even the rides at Disneyland, the best ones, have a sense of progression and involve the patron in a simple story.

I got into my first story meeting with Walt by accident, and I'll never forget it. It took place on a hot morning in September 1935. By then, I had been working at the studio for half a year and had never seen Walt, except that time in the men's room and brief glimpses of him in the halls and on the "lot".

At the time I accidentally encountered him, I was working on gags for a picture about broken dolls repairing themselves in clever ways in order to give orphan children a surprise on Christmas morning.[6] I had a couple of good ideas, and decided it was time to bypass Hogsworth and see Sligh.

Walt's office was in an upstairs wing of the main building, and one morning about eight-thirty I went up to see him, but he hadn't come in yet. Walking back down the carpeted hall to the stairway, I passed a story room where a young fellow was seated in a chair studying a long storyboard filled with sketches. When I entered the room, he jumped to his feet and quickly turned the board to the wall in order to hide his story from me. Then, as if he had done nothing unusual, we shook hands and introduced ourselves. He was a short, ruddy-faced fellow with curly black hair, and his name was Pophoff. I knew well that all storymen, striving for credit, regarded fellow workers as potential thieves. Pophoff seemed nervous and anxious to get back to work. I left and he quickly shut the door.

The door of a room nearby was open, and two large storyboards covered with sketches hung on the wall, one above the other. Animated cartoon stories were not written but told with sketches, and the storyman had to explain his story after he had drawn it out for Walt. Evidently a meeting was scheduled, for two rows of chairs had been placed in front of the boards.

This was hallowed ground, and looking over a man's storyboards when he was absent was regarded as gagnapping, a crime equivalent to cheating a blind widow. But what harm could I do? I entered the room, large and well-furnished except for the chairs. They looked like rejects from a WPA[7] project. I scanned the boards quickly and saw the story was about mountain climbing. It opened with Mickey and Donald Duck climbing a cliff tied together by a rope. The end of the rope was tied around the waist of Pluto, the dog, leaving him dangling helplessly in space. Right off, I saw a little personality gag for Pluto and decided to sketch it up, leave it on one of the chairs, and be gone before the meeting started. I took a sheet of animation paper from a stack on the desk behind me, and, sitting down, became absorbed in my drawing.

Suddenly, a lean man of about fifty strolled into the room. He had a sun-dried face and curly, white hair. He rolled a cigar around in his mouth and grinned at me, crow's feet crinkling away in long lines from the corners of his pale blue eyes. We introduced ourselves, and he said his name was Strayshott.

Suddenly, I remembered what I had heard about him. He had a slow way of telling a story and was said to drag it out, chuckling all the time. He used to get Walt's goat, for Walt was an impatient man. By the time Strayshott had reached the second line of sketches on the first storyboard, Walt would be studying the last sketch on the last board. Strayshott had a funny style of drawing, and his room, it was said, connected to that of Sligh. All gags submitted (except mine, seemingly) landed on Sligh's desk first. The rumor went around that Sligh and Strayshott evaluated them together, and Strayshott would redraw the best gags in his funny style and pin them upon his storyboards for study. Walt dropped by Sligh's office regularly, and Sligh would steer him into Strayshott's adjoining room. Then Strayshott explained the gags and would get to laughing so hard he forgot to tell Walt whose gags they were, a natural oversight in the excitement of the moment.

It was rumored that Walt's execs pounded the "Three Musketeers" theme into the artists—"All for one and one for all"—a happy family working for Walt and a great future. I was told that long before I came to the studio, the storymen had discovered things weren't just that way. They said Walt didn't give a damn whose gag it was, as long as it improved the picture, and a spirit of secrecy had developed among the storymen. Generosity vanished, and, gag-wise, they became tighter than a gnat's ass.

Strayshott asked me what I was doing, and I said I was working on gags for a Christmas picture about broken dolls and had come up to see Mr. Sligh, but he wasn't in. "Just leave 'em on his desk," Strayshott said. I thanked him and said I couldn't resist the open door, and, glancing through the story, saw a gag for the dog Pluto. Strayshott was about to look at it when a shattering cough was heard. He chuckled, "That'll be Walt or Clem Longshanks. They've both got God-awful coughs."

Just then, a short, pot-bellied, middle-aged fellow walked in. His sparse brown hair was parted in the middle. He was apparently an old-timer in the business, and it didn't take long to tell he had bronchitis, and bad. Several other fellows drifted in. I learned later one of them was Diddle. He smoked a pipe and asked, in a relaxed manner, "Is this where the execution takes place?" He dropped into a chair next to the yellow wicker chair. Then a thin, tall fellow strolled in. He had on a white shirt and a fore-in-hand tie that seemed too short for him. He had a red face, a shoe button nose, a long upper lip, and a receding chin. His black hair was combed straight back from a low forehead. His murky eyes coasted around the room taking me in, and I noticed they were empty, devoid of any feeling. He was greeted with "Hi, Si." So that was Sligh, and I was seeing him for the first time.

I started to leave the room when a smiling young girl breezed in carrying a steno machine. I stepped aside for her, just as Walt charged through the door. He brushed past me and slumped into the wicker chair amidst a chorus of "Good morning, Walt." He ignored the greetings: eyebrows arched, he was glancing around abruptly and shot a glance at me, as if to say who the hell are you? Then he turned back to the storyboards. Apparently, he took in everything.

Once again, I was struck by his resemblance to a Spaniard. He had a high-bridged nose, a small black mustache, and thick, straight, dark hair. But I knew by now that he was of Scottish-Irish descent. He wore dark slacks and a dark blue, short-sleeved jersey with narrow horizontal stripes of a lighter hue. Although he was slightly built and of medium height, he was large-boned with the physique of a guy who lifted weights. His forearms were muscular, and he had big boney hands with long sturdy fingers, and those fingers were never still during the meeting, plucking at loose pieces of wicker or drumming impatiently on the arm of his chair. He glanced around the group and said, "Alright, Clem, let's get on with it."

Longshanks wheezed out a bronchial blast and pointed to the first drawing with a wooden pointer. He began describing the actions of Mickey and Donald climbing the mountain. Suddenly, Walt interrupted, "We want a little fast music to begin with and a blend of yodeling from Mickey and the Duck."

"Good, Walt," said Longshanks. He had barely resumed when Walt cut in again. "Every time they drive their picks into the mountain they should do a leap frog effect, like a spring, and yodel right after it."

"Right." Longshanks had reached the third sketch. Walt frowned.

"What about Pluto?" he said. "He's got to do something. He can't hang around like a sack of potatoes."

A thoughtful silence fell over the room. This was one of the most important moments of my life. An idea popped into my mind. I was still making only $15 a week. Some of the fellows had told me the only way to get ahead was to impress Walt, personally.

Here he was, and now was my chance to do it. Nobody here was going to do it for me. I listened to my voice break the silence, as if it was the voice of a stranger. "What if a little bush grows on the side of the cliff and Pluto tries to sniff it but gets yanked away."

Walt came to life. He swung around to face me. "That's good!" he said. I felt like I'd won the sweepstakes. A lot of grim smiles surrounded me, but I ignored them and resolved to come up with anything else that seemed funny.

"We can use this gag a couple of times," Walt was saying.

"Every time Pluto tries to sniff a bush or a tree he gets yanked up. He's helpless."

Sligh said, "We can use it for a running gag."

Walt was talking directly to me. "That's good dog personality stuff. That's the type of gag we need around here."

Then he looked back at the boards, and I glanced at Sligh. He was snow-white under the eyes. I began to sweat.

Meanwhile, Longshanks went on with his story. "Mickey is up first and he pulls up the duck. Then both of them pull Pluto up and the duck ties Pluto to a boulder." Then I interrupted him, "Could Pluto look back over the edge of the cliff and make a frightened 'take'? He backs up and puts his paws over his eyes."

Walt laughed for the first time. "He's frightened. He cringes."

Longshanks said the duck had gone off to pick edelweiss while Mickey hunted for eagle eggs. He had a lot of stuff drawn up for Walt to shoot at, but Walt ignored the storyboards. He turned to the group, and, without hesitating, went through a non-stop funny routine. I was impressed. He was a hell of a gag man. He jumped to his feet and went on like this: "Mickey starts picking up eagle eggs in excitement. He's real happy, then a dark shadow comes into the scene; Mickey looks up and sees the mother eagle sitting on top of a boulder, watching him. Mickey gives an embarrassed chuckle and starts putting the eggs back in the nest, one at a time. All the time, he keeps an eye on the mother eagle. She watches him with a fierce expression. He puts the last egg into the nest, but drops it. A little eagle pops out. Mickey tries to pat it.

"'Nice little guy,' he says, but the eagle nips his finger. Mickey lets out a yell and the mother eagle zooms down at him. He fires eagle eggs at her, and as he throws them, they pop open and little eagles come sailing out. They attack Mickey. He covers his head and shoves them into Pluto's scene. All the time, the old girl is on the rock. She's urging her little eagles on. Pluto comes to Mickey's aid, running around the boulder with the rock he's tied to bouncing along behind him."

Then Walt fell silent and slumped back into his chair.

He fished in his pocket and pulled out a crumpled pack of Lucky Strikes. Diddle, seated beside him, held a match while the rest of the men were saying, "That's great, Walt...funny stuff." Everything he said was fresh and funny and in continuity. That was the marvel of it. I knew then he wasn't Walt Disney for nothing. He seemed to be talking to himself. "What do we do with the Duck?"

"The Duck's collecting flowers and singing," said Longshanks.

"He can't just pick flowers. I want him to do something funny," said Walt, impatiently.

I had it. "He's got a bunch of edelweiss; just as he holds it up to admire it, a little mountain goat pops out from behind a rock and chomps the flowers off, leaving the surprised Duck holding the stems."

"He gets madder than hell," cried Walt.

Everybody began tossing out gag ideas, and we developed a lot of back-and-forth stuff between the little goat and the angry Duck.

Walt got hot again. "Another little goat joins the first little goat and they come at the Duck from different directions and try to butt him. He picks up a rock and holds it between them and they butt it. The Duck laughs and then finds he's facing the old man goat."

Walt stopped again.

"The old man goat butts the Duck up the side of a cliff; he's kayoed," suggested Longshanks. "We come back to him later." He ended with a wheezy cough.

"I wish we had something better than that," said Walt.

I was so excited about being in a story meeting with Walt that I was thinking myself crazy. I stood up without realizing it. "The old man goat butts the Duck up an ice hill. He slides down and gets butted up again."

Longshanks interrupted me. "What's so funny about that?"

"Wait a minute, I'm not finished," I cried. "After getting butted up the hill a couple of times the Duck loses his temper and butts the old man goat."

"Too corny," said Sligh.

Walt swung around to face him, "Corny? What's corny about it?" he cried. "The Duck's got a helluva temper, hasn't he? So he turns around and runs straight at the old man goat, who comes straight at him. We cut back and forth like two trains coming together, and, BLAM, the old goat flies out of the scene and lands flat on his back, dizzy as hell."

Everybody cracked up, but Walt scowled. "Maybe we're getting too straight around here. Maybe we need to go a little farther."

I could feel everybody in the room tighten. I looked at my watch; a quarter to twelve. The group seemed restless and tired, but Walt was just getting steamed up. He was able to do the whole story by himself. He didn't need any help; just a couple of cigar store Indians to bounce his stuff off of. He described everything clearly as if it had taken place on a picture screen in his mind. With everybody itching to go to lunch, Walt was hot.

"We go back to Pluto chasing the little eagle," he said.

"The rock he's tied to bouncing along behind him. The eagle flies off the edge of the cliff and Pluto saves himself by grabbing a bush with his teeth. The big rock he's tied to bounces past him, goes over the edge, and yanks Pluto after it. He bounces from ledge to ledge and the rock lands first at the bottom in the snow. Pluto 'BONGS' into it and is knocked out cold. Cut to a little doghouse with a Red Cross flag flying from the top. A big St. Bernard sticks his head out and comes over to Pluto, half-buried in snow, and pulls him out by the tail. Pluto's stiff and blue with the cold. He clatters around like a plate on the ice. The St. Bernard turns the spigot on his brandy keg with his mouth. He's very matter-offact about it."

Walt went on in a rush, his eyes vacant as if he actually saw the picture animating before him and he was simply describing what he saw. He told how Pluto changed color after swallowing the liquor. A series of red circles formed on his blue stomach and got bigger and bigger until Pluto was his own color again. Then Pluto became drunk. I suggested, "He licks the St. Bernard's jowls."

"Yes," Walt said. "The St. Bernard is very dignified. He turns his head away, disgusted, he can't stand the fumes. We cut back to Mickey, the Duck, and the eagles." Walt fell back into his chair and fished for another cigarette. Again Diddle held a match for him. Walt took a long drag, followed by a hollow cough. "We don't have to bring them all back together again," he said, becoming thoughtful. "They could just finish their individual pieces of business and we could end on Pluto and the St. Bernard."

I said, "What if Mickey and the Duck were chased off the cliff by the eagles and fall down through the roof of the St. Bernard's house?"

"That will tie it all together," exclaimed Walt. "They come up out of the wrecked roof and look offstage and hear singing. We cut to the dogs at the end. They're both drunk, howling and yodeling together."

Sligh thought "Sweet Adeline" would be appropriate.

Walt frowned at him. "No, let's get something more in keeping with this type of picture. At the end, both dogs lean together for a long chord. Get Barker to do the dog voices. The St. Bernard should have a deep bass voice and Pluto a high one. After Barker does both voices, we'll dub them together."

Then Walt went back over the whole story from beginning to end, never hesitating, adding new things as he went along. His mind seemed to be a kaleidoscope of ideas forever changing, sending new images to him. I think his mind was something he couldn't turn off if he had wanted to. A hard driver, not very interested, perhaps, in the ones being driven, only interested in improving the stories.

Walt stood up. I looked at my watch again. This time it was ten after one o'clock. "You've got a lot of stuff here now, Clem," he said. "Let's get busy and tie it up. Build that Duck stuff. Show him always starting things. I want Mickey to get going with that eagle business before we cut to the Duck."

While Walt was talking, Strayshott suggested Pluto's nose flashing on and off like a light globe.

"I would like to see the whites of their eyes show red," added Sligh.

"Let's have a final meeting next week," said Walt, and strode out of the room.

"Have you got it all down?" Longshanks asked the secretary.

"I think so," she said.

"When can I get the notes?"

"This afternoon."

Longshanks stared forlornly at his storyboards. He groaned, "Christ, I'll have to draw the sonofabitchin' thing all over again."

"How about a sketch man to help? Strayshott can give you a lift," suggested Sligh.

Longshanks reacted as if he'd been stabbed. "No, no, thanks just the same, Si. I'll slug it out myself."

Clem Longshanks didn't want Strayshott's funny sketches covering his storyboards. He knew from long experience that by next week Walt would have forgotten whose gags were whose, and Strayshott would get the credit. I remembered again hearing it said all Walt cared about was the final result.

Strayshott and Sligh were leaving for lunch, and I caught up with them. "You had a good idea in the meeting, Homer," said Strayshott, between puffs on his cigar. I thanked him and asked Mr. Sligh if I could show him my broken doll gags after lunch.

His face was expressionless. "No need to," he said. "Just keep turning them in to Hogsworth. When he gets a big enough batch, he brings them up to me."

He was an old smoothy. "Okay," I replied, and watched the two go down the stairs together. It would be a long Siberian winter before I got into another meeting with Walt. Nevertheless, I was elated. I had made an impression on him, and something was bound to happen.

It did. That afternoon I was called up into Hogsworth's office. With his usual superior manner he said, "We're raising you to $25 a week."

In Walt's cast of characters, none was more popular than Donald Duck. I think he appeared first in *The Wise Little Hen*, but I thought his second picture, *Orphan's Benefit*, was a lot funnier.

In this one, the Duck strode onto the stage and Mickey announced he would recite "Little Boy Blue". When he came to "come blow your horn", a crowd of Mickey's orphans in the gallery gave him the raspberry. Every time he tried to repeat the poem, he was hooted and jeered by the crowd, and, losing his temper, wanted to fight everybody. A long cane with a hook on the end of it zipped out from the wings and yanked him off stage. The Duck, animated by Grout, was an immediate hit with the public, and Donald Duck was the name decided upon by Walt. He immediately began a search for a suitable voice. One day, he heard of a young fellow who drove a little milk wagon drawn by Shetland ponies and who visited schools, where he gave imitations of animal voices and bird calls. Walt had him in for an audition and discovered the voice of Donald Duck. The Duck became so popular Walt signed with King Features to feature him in a daily newspaper comic strip.[8]

I was given the task of doing the gags, and an artist drew the finished strip. It caught on, but I was unhappy because I wanted to work in the Story Department. Walt heard about it and agreed to transfer me back if I could train someone to take my place, and, happily, a very good prospect turned up. We worked together, and soon he was able to take over gags for the strip and I was back on pictures.[9]

While working in the bungalow on comic strip gags, I became acquainted with a middle-aged, silent, gloomy Englishman who inked the *Good Housekeeping* page and who also inked on the *Mickey Mouse* comic strip. I thought of him as "Gloomy Gus". He brought his lunch every day and always ate a small can of Libby's fruit cocktail for dessert. Day after day, it was fruit cocktail. The fellows couldn't let this go on, and managed to get the can of fruit cocktail and fix the label to another can of a Libby product so that when "Gloomy Gus" opened his can of fruit cocktail it would contain succotash, green beans, hash, anything but fruit cocktail. The fellow was amazed and told everybody about the mistake Libby's had made, and it was suggested to him that he go across the street to the market where he was a steady customer and threaten to sue both the market and Libby's for the mistake. The market manager was in on the gag and promised to take it up with Libby's at once. But "Gloomy" finally caught on, and, to him, there was nothing "bloody well funny" about it.

A couple of months later, he left Disney for greener fields, if there were any at that time.[10]

After returning to the Story Department, I attended a meeting in Projection Room #4, where Walt was reviewing a partially animated cartoon. Links, one of the best directors in the studio, was directing the picture, and Walt, who didn't like the stuff, was chewing him out. The room was in complete darkness. Suddenly, a girl with a decided Texas drawl spoke up, "You-all can't talk that way to him!"

Walt shouted, "Lights!" Then turned around and bellowed, "Who said that?"

"I did, you old meany," said a pretty girl with a Texas drawl.

"Who are you anyway?" demanded Walt, "and what's your name?"

"I'm Mr. Links' secretary," said the girl.

Walt's eyebrows met in a menacing arc. "I don't think you are in a position that calls for comments of any kind when I'm reviewing a picture. Let's get on with the damn thing."

The room went black again, and the rough picture appeared on the screen.

Links' secretary's return to Texas was not overly long delayed.

Chapter Three

Before being employed by Walt Disney, I had spent ten years at sea as a lowly apprentice on sailing ships, rising to a Second Mate's berth on steamships. So far, I had been successful in what I set out to do—become a sea captain. But a sudden accident in Colombo [Ceylon, now Sri Lanka] changed my life, and when I recovered, the old Robert Dollar Steamship Lines offered me a position in their Shanghai offices. After two years there, they transferred me to Hong Kong and later to Singapore. The office in Singapore was in the Hong Kong and Shanghai Bank building, and the staff consisted of three white men and several Chinese and Malay clerks.

On a hot December morning in 1927, the manager handed me a decoded cablegram from our executive offices in San Francisco. It read:

"Have Brightman report New York first available transportation."

I had represented our Shanghai office when thousands of thirty-pound tin-plate cans of frozen Chinese eggs had been loaded into the refer holds of our round-the-world steamers, and 58 days later, in off-loading at Boston and New York, a lot of shipments turned out defrosted. The consignees had filed a chain of lawsuits against the company, claiming negligence in not keeping the refer at the proper temperature. In the back of my mind, I carried the thought that someday I might be called upon, and now I was sure this was why I was suddenly being sent to New York.

The manager said, "When can you leave?"

"Any time." I always traveled light. Square up a few "chits" and I could be on my way.

I left Singapore the next day on board the *President Van Buren* bound for New York via the Suez Canal.

In New York, I had numerous meetings with the law firm representing the Dollar Line, and one week I took the train to Chicago to visit with my folks, whom I hadn't seen in over eight years. They thought I looked pale and drawn, and I had a bad cough. The folks' doctor sent me to a noted tuberculosis specialist, and, after a long examination of my chest, he said, "You'll be a memory in six months." The next day I telephoned New York, soft-pedaling the doctor's prediction, because I didn't want to believe I could have the bad luck to be laid up.

Since extensive medical tests were necessary, the company decided my testimony in the pending lawsuits could be taken by deposition in Chicago. When my testimony had been completed and sent to the company, I expected they would no longer require my services and terminate me. But I was never one to worry and feel sorry for myself. I had a sort of Mr. Micawber philosophy; "something was bound to turn up". And it did! Out of the blue came a message. The company would grant me immediately a four-month paid vacation, and in addition, continue my salary for another six months. If by then I was unable to return to the Orient, they would be obliged to replace me. God! How I loved the Robert Dollar organization! You didn't find many employers like that.

My doctor gave much of his valuable time working for free as the medical director of a sanatorium located in the country west of Chicago. It was a charitable institution for Westside Chicago Jews, but they had a small wing to accommodate a few gentiles who were able to pay. The cost was only $84 a month, and I considered myself lucky to be accepted. After almost 20 months under sanatorium care, I was pronounced an arrested case.

In those days, rest and fresh air was the prescribed treatment for TB. We spent all our days and nights in outdoor screened-in porches shivering through long winter nights, often in 18-degrees-below-zero weather, without the benefit of electric blankets, and sweltering in humid summer heat, as air conditioning hadn't arrived in those days.

About a year after entering the "san", good news came from the New York attorneys. Because of my testimony, the lawsuits had been settled out of court in our favor.

After becoming an arrested TB patient, I asked the doctor how soon I could return to Singapore. "Never!" was his abrupt reply. The news hit me like a typhoon, and he added that going back to the sea was out of the question. From now on, I must look forward to a sedentary life. From now on, if I wanted to survive, I must be slow to take offense and "never run for a streetcar".

His good advice came in the middle of the Great Depression, when soup lines were easier to find than jobs. I was on a "lee shore" with no prospects of getting off it.

Although the doctor urged me to stay in the Chicago area where he could keep an eye on me, I thought gray, smoky Chicago was too depressing, and so I cleared out for Arizona where I could soak up sunshine.

Arriving in Tucson, I found room and board for $50 a month with a farm family from Iowa. They had moved West for the same reason I had, but the father had died and his eldest son was on his way to the same end.

My landlady was the fattest woman I had ever seen. She must have weighed 300 pounds. She thudded about the house, her heavy tread sending vibrations along the floor and jarring pictures on the walls. On my first day, she waddled ahead of me along the hall, her big rear end working up and down like pistons. The doorway to my room was so narrow she had to squeeze in sideways. When I had joined her, there was hardly standing room, for my new accommodations were no larger than a third mate's cabin on a freighter.

My landlady was good-natured, and at mealtime sat enthroned at the head of the table, heaping the plates with generous helpings of boiled beef, boiled potatoes, and boiled cabbage, sloshing vinegar over the food, her face glistening with perspiration. Then she smiled at everyone and said Grace. At first I thought all that vinegar was what got to her husband, because it was as routine at meals as pepper and salt.

Once settled, I began to think of my urgent need to begin a new life. What would it be? My question was answered when I saw an ad in a magazine reading, "BE A HUMOROUS ILLUSTRATOR". That would be a quiet, pleasant way to earn my living. The catch was, I couldn't draw. But, reading on, I was assured that "Russell Patterson" would teach me by mail in "only 20 easy lessons for just $35, payable in advance".

The next day I sent a money order to New York, and a week later received a package containing 20 glossy plates of the master's work together with 20 mimeographed sheets of instructions. After completing each lesson, I was to mail it back to Mr. Patterson for his criticism. Upon completing the course, my graduation present would be a beautiful original drawing signed by the master himself. I never received the beautiful drawing, because I gave up on the course after completing the fourth lesson, realizing I never could imitate Mr. Patterson's spidery, pretty girl technique.

But I never gave up sketching. I worked all day, every day, at it, and soon discovered I had some natural talent to draw funny cartoons, and, through trial and error, learned how to submit them to magazines. I began to sell now and then, and I never became discouraged by many rejections.

One winter evening, I sat on the worn couch in the living room and was about to doze off when my landlady barged in. On the table in front of the couch was an old portable typewriter. She sat down on a little stool with her back to me and announced she was going to write a letter "back home to Iowa", and began pecking at the keys with one fat forefinger, her big rear end sagged over the sides of the stool like a loosely filled sack of grain. I thought she made a funny picture, and, opening my sketch book, I made a quick sketch of her. A loud wheezy sigh was a hint that she had finished her letter. I closed my sketch book and, hiding it behind me, pretended to be asleep. After the floor stopped creaking and her door slammed shut, I hurried to my room and made a final drawing.

The next day I mailed it off to the Post Scripts editor of the *Saturday Evening Post*. They bought it and asked me to try them again.

During breakfast the next morning, I said enthusiastically that I had sold a cartoon to the *Saturday Evening Post*, and my landlady asked me when it would appear. I suddenly wished I'd kept my mouth shut, because a little boy delivered the *Post* to me every week and my landlady always took it in, and I was afraid she might see the cartoon. Weeks later, I heard a shout come from the front door area. "How many do you want?"

"How many what?" I cried. Then, suddenly realizing my cartoon was in that issue of the *Post*, I hurried to the front door to be confronted by my angry landlady. She stood with a copy of the *Post* in hand, folded back, and pointing a shaking finger at a picture. Her face was a fiery red, and her jowls quivered with rage.

"You made a nasty drawing of me," she cried, indignantly, "and I'm going to sue you for every dime you've got!" I didn't want to lose what little money I had left, and so, looking doubtfully at the drawing, shook my head. "That is not you!" I lied.

"It is too me and you know it is!"

"Do you mean to tell me that you look like that cartoon?" I demanded, feigning amazement.

"Don't I?" Hopefully.

"Absolutely not!" Firmly. "Please don't be ridiculous. That drawing is no more like you than a p--." I was about to say pig, but corrected myself in time, "...than a-a-a pigeon. It's just a cartoon I made up. You don't look anything like that, a bit!"

"That's really not me then?"

"Of course not!" I lied, but it was her to a "T". "Well..." she fluffed up her hair a few times, then waddled over to the couch and dropped onto it with a "twang" as a spring snapped. While she sighed with relief, I eased myself out of the room.

I finally decided Tucson was not the ideal place for an unknown cartoonist.

My health improved steadily, and on a blast furnace day in August I departed by carpool for Chicago. I found a room there in a boarding house serving two meals a day: breakfast and supper. The gimlet-eyed landlady presided over the table, and I was served food in proportion to the amount of rent paid, the least in the house.

My room was a partitioned-off corner of the third-floor attic, and I awoke in the morning in a pool of sweat after a night of Chicago's high humidity. But every morning, rain or shine, I set out for the Loop (downtown Chicago), and made the rounds of art directors in department stores and ad agencies. Now and then, they assigned me a cartoon. With my submissions to magazines I was able to pay rent and add to my portfolio of clippings. No work of a steady nature came my way, but I struggled on with a sinking feeling that I was nearing the end of a one-way street.

Some months passed in this manner, and my spirits fell like autumn leaves from the trees.

While browsing through a secondhand book store late in December 1934, I came across an old issue of *Fortune* magazine.[11] A long article gave an account of Walt Disney and his studio, a mecca for artists and idea men. Instantly, I knew that was where I wanted to be, and wrote a letter to Walt Disney. Despite a discouraging reply from his secretary, I armed myself with a letter of introduction to a Disney animator from a political cartoonist friend of his and set out for Hollywood, via the Southern Pacific chair car route.

Chapter Four

All big story meetings with Walt were held in Projection Room #4, popularly referred to as Sweat Box 4. Here, 20 or 30 storymen, animators, and layout men gathered with Walt, while the nervous storyman, hoping to get laughs, pointed to his sketches and acted them out as he went along.

The first story I was responsible for was *The Fox Hunt*, and the meeting was held on a May night in 1937. Before the meeting, I made sure none of my drawings had been rearranged, as it was considered a good gag (but not for the storyman) to shift his drawings around so they didn't make sense. Someone would sneak in and do the job just before the meeting began.

Everybody would be in on the gag except Walt, who glowered at the poor victim, under the impression he wasn't able to tell a story.

The trick had been played on me, but I had my sketches back in order, and when Walt arrived I was ready to tell the story. Mickey was in charge, Donald Duck was Master of the Hounds. The rest of the cast consisted of Minnie Mouse, Horace Horse Collar, Clarabelle Cow, and Goofy, all mounted on horses.

The hounds dragged Donald through fences tangling him up in the leashes. He lost his temper and cussed them. A large pond had a tree growing in the middle of it, and the hounds dragged him into the pond. A string of bubbles headed for the tree and circled it and stopped. A flock of bubbles surfaced and resulted in a lot of laughs. Later, Goofy and his horse missed a water jump and disappeared with a big splash, and when the horse surfaced and climbed up the bank, his hind feet were in Goofy's riding boots. They were back to back and some funny business resulted. The story seemed to be going over very well, and at the climax, Donald saw the tip of a tail sticking up out of a stump. He ran over, grabbed the tail, and shouted, "I've got him! I've got him!" The riders skidded into the scene, and, seeing the tail belonged to a skunk, vanished in a flash.

Donald turned to see what he had pulled out of the stump and vanished, too, leaving the skunk in mid-air.

I was acting the part of Donald, and in my excitement tripped and stumbled backward. It was quite a stumble, because it took me out of the room and across the hall and into a room where an animator was working. I crashed into the animator's desk and knocked the top off and the glass shattered. The animator, his chair, and I crashed into a corner. I was sure I "was "dead" and didn't even think I would go back into the story meeting. Then loud laughter exploded and I peered hesitantly around the door, and Walt motioned for me to come in. That was one of the few times I saw him laugh heartily, for he was not given to it.

The next day, I signed my first contract, a three-year deal with yearly options, and my salary had been increased from $45 to $70 a week. I had impressed Walt again.

Sometimes it was hard to figure out what would impress Walt, and I remember one of those times. A story crew—Strayshott, Duddleham, and Fluk—were working on a story they were excited about, and tentatively titled *Clock Cleaners*. The plot: Mickey, Goofy, and Donald ran a watch repair business from a small car. A sign on top of their car announced they were running a special and would clean any clock for one dollar.

Pete, the "heavy", stopped their car and gave them a job to clean a clock for him. He made sure they charged only ONE dollar and paid it. Then he pointed out the clock, located on the tower of a sixty-story building.

When they tried to back out, Pete threatened violence. The three had no choice, and were soon at work high above the street, cleaning pendulums, springs, weights. Human figures made of iron came out of doors on a track and hammered the big bell. A lady figure came out and Goofy, who was cleaning the bell, bowed and tipped his hat, and she klunked him on the head with her hammer. A stork had built a nest in one of the gears, and every time they threw him out he sailed back in again. Mickey had trouble cleaning the face of the huge clock high above the street. I thought they had good stuff.

I had been assigned to work on gags with the story crew, and started work on the day they had a meeting with Walt. Strayshott told the story in his slow chuckling style. During the telling, I noticed Walt had moved from the front row of seats to the back row and slumped into a seat with his feet on the back of the seat in front of him. Strayshott finally finished, and Walt, scowling at all of us, slammed his pork-pie hat on his head, said "Shit!", and stormed out of the room. We looked at each other in dismay. Strayshott, his forehead wrinkled like an old tin roof after a hurricane, picked up his soggy cigar and said, "You know, I don't think he liked it."

Chapter Five

"Get your hands off that CRUMIUM!" Suggs' booming voice startled me, and I snatched my hand back from the chrome bumper of his shiny, new, black limousine, as if I had accidentally touched a hot stove. He came over, pulling a handkerchief from the back pocket of his khaki pants and carefully wiped away an imaginary spot. So Suggs had made another down payment on a big car. It would soon be repossessed, and he would be driving his old Model T again. But that never worried him. While he had the car, he took loving care of it, for then he was no longer a poorly paid gag man, but, as he put it, "a man of means". Driving his shining car to work every morning, he went out of his way to pass slowly in front of big plate glass display windows in order to admire his reflection in them.

Suggs weighed 275 pounds and stood five feet ten. He was on his way to early baldness and his beetling brow, beady little eyes, and jutting jaw gave him the appearance of a clean-shaven prehistoric man.

I looked at my watch. The lunch period was over. Time to get back to work. I left Suggs gazing in silent admiration at his spotless car, and, entering the building, I went upstairs.

Walt, in one of his personnel shuffles, had teamed Pophoff and me together, and we shared the same office on the second floor.

Suggs' car was parked directly below our window, and Pophoff looked down on it while I told him of Suggs' violent reaction when I touched his precious chrome bumper.

We decided to "fix" up his car, and so Pophoff went over to the Ink and Paint Department and borrowed a jar of white opaque water color paint and a brush. While one of us kept a lookout, the other painted signs all over Suggs' gleaming black beauty. When we had covered every available space, it was apparent his car was "For Sale!" "Sheriff's sale!" "Owner forced to sell!" "A steal!" "Take me away for ten bucks down!" "No monthly payments!" "You name it—you've got it!" "The buy of a lifetime!" "Our special this week only!" "Owner going out of town—needs cash!"

Looking down on our handiwork, we couldn't stop laughing. Finally, we returned to our desks and our assignment on the *Snow White* bed-building sequence. We had just settled down when the door flew open, and, framed in the doorway, stood Suggs, silent and menacing. I started to say something, but he cut me off. "Shut up!" he snapped. My desk was nearest to the door and he jumped over, and, grabbing my hand, minutely examined each of my fingers, then, dropping my hand, picked up the other one, carefully examining it. Then he turned to Pophoff and did the same thing. His examination completed, he glared at us and said, "If there had been one speck of white paint under your fingernails, you'd both be dead by now!" He left, slamming the door so hard the glass panel shattered. A couple of minutes later, Walt came along, treading in the broken glass. He had H. G. Wells and Charlie Chaplin in tow. All three stared through the big hole in the glass door. "What the hell happened?" demanded Walt.

"It must have been the wind," I suggested lamely.

Charlie Chaplin smiled. "In this business you've got to relax now and then," he said, understandingly. Walt never could appreciate horseplay on studio time, and, while Wells and Chaplin grinned at us, Walt gave us a disgusted look, and the three of them moved on. Walt was probably giving them a tour of the studio.[12] When Pophoff went home that night, he discovered someone had let all the air out of his tires—with an ice pick. Fortunately for me, I didn't own a car.

An animator from New York, an old-timer in the business, worked in the office next to mine. Every night before leaving he mooched a cigarette and never repaid it. Finally, in desperation, I decided to break him of the habit. I bought a cigarette bomb in a trick store on Hollywood Boulevard and inserted it deep into the cigarette he would be sure to borrow from me before going home. He did, and I walked with him to the Red Car line.

Quite a large crowd waited in the safety zone. The animator fished in his pocket and pulled out my cigarette, lighted it, and took exactly three big drags before it exploded. Everybody in the loading zone broke into laughter at the sight of his blackened face. When the car rolled to a stop, he boarded it. The car seemed to be too crowded for me, so I waited for the next one. The fellow never spoke to me again, but he didn't borrow any more of my cigarettes, either.

The Band Concert featured Mickey Mouse, and the setting was a park where Mickey and his band were giving a concert. A big cyclone came along and sucked up the band. It continued to play, with Mickey directing, and was finally strewn over the ground in various funny positions, as the cyclone moved on, leaving the band playing furiously.

An Hispanic animator was assigned to animate Mickey Mouse. He got into the right mood using the Actor's Studio method of animating by marching up and down in a drum major's uniform. Walt saw him strutting around the halls and told him to get to work. A day or two later, Walt ordered him to bring his animation up to his office.

The animator took a stack of 500 animation pages up to Walt and told him this was the scene. Walt smiled; he was happy at this prodigious output. But, as he leafed through the pages, he found that only the top page had a drawing. All the rest were blank. Walt went white. "Out!" he shouted, pointing to the door. The animator never worked for Disney again, but he had no trouble finding work. He was one of the most gifted animators in the business.

With increasing production the studio became crowded, and Walt was forced to find more space. He acquired an old, vacant, two-story apartment building adjoining the parking lot on Hyperion Avenue. A section of the wall was knocked out to create a passageway, and many of the Shorts Department personnel, including me, were moved into the new building.

What a cold, gloomy place it was. Plaster had fallen off the walls, exposing the laths, and the only heat came from unvented little gas heaters attached to the main valves in the walls by rubber tubes. At first our windows were without blinds or drapes, adding to the abandoned appearance, and the walls were blank except for our storyboards stacked against them. Battered desks and a few old chairs for meetings made up the only furniture on the uncarpeted floors.

In our new quarters there wasn't the "heavy, heavy hangs over your head" atmosphere of the main building. We felt free to work and have fun, as Walt was rarely able to make his surprise visits because somebody was bound to see him crossing the parking lot and sound the alarm. When he showed up, everybody was hard at work.

It was not too long after the move that Pophoff's old high school teacher from the Midwest paid him a visit. Unfortunately, he was now in the "low rent" district, no longer in his comfortable room in the main building. Nevertheless, he was anxious to impress his teacher with the progress he had made since leaving high school.

Suggs, on the spur of the moment, came up with a plan to impress the teacher, and we set to work while Pophoff was showing her around the studio and taking her to lunch.

Old magazine pictures of pin-up girls, along with notes, were pinned to Pophoff's storyboards. "All my love, Vicky." "All the way any day, Margo." "How about a party tonight, you old devil! Kitty." Pophoff's dirty shorts and socks, from his daily noon-time games, were tacked to his storyboards. Empty beer bottles littered the floor.

About an hour later, Pophoff ushered the dignified old lady into his room and closed the door. His apologetic dialogue and nervous laugh echoed through the empty room. "Heh, heh, heh; guys play dirty tricks; heh, heh, heh, get even, heh, heh, heh."

The door opened and his old teacher came out, her pince-nez glasses quivering on her prominent nose. She was consulting her watch. She was already late...her friend was picking her up at the front gate... no, it wouldn't be necessary to accompany her, she would do very nicely. She thanked Pophoff for a pleasant visit. Now he must get on with his WORK. She emphasized that word and left. Pophoff stood in the doorway, red-faced and jerking at his collar with a nervous forefinger, while Suggs, who had stepped into the hall, watched the old lady totter down the stairs. "Was that your school teacher?" he asked innocently.

Several days later, Suggs, homeward bound, got into his old Model T, failing to notice a metal wheelbarrow had been jammed in the half-opened trunk and filled to the brim with water. When he revved up the engine, water sloshed all over him and his car. The heavy wheelbarrow could not be removed until the water had been bailed out. Suggs was late getting home that night.

A distance of about four feet separated our new quarters from a similar old but still occupied apartment building. The people in the apartment next to Suggs' second-floor window had a rowdy boy. He had no one to play with, which was just as well, as he made enough noise by himself. His only play area was in the narrow space between the two buildings. One summer morning, when I dropped in, he was making a hellish racket playing fire engine. Suddenly, Suggs, always impetuous, grabbed a five-gallon bottle of drinking water that had just been delivered and dropped it out of his second-floor window. Fortunately, it missed the boy, but shattered, dousing him with water. The drenched boy screamed bloody murder and his mother, looking out of her window in alarm, came face to face with Suggs, who hadn't time to duck out of sight. She accused him of trying to kill her boy. Suggs tried to apologize, claiming he was attempting to put the bottle on the stand, when it slipped from his hands and fell out the window. But the mother, a coarse sort of woman, accused him in vulgar terms of being a killer and charged over to the main building demanding to see Walt. Her son followed her, screaming "killer, killer, killer". In a surprisingly short time, the telephone rang and Suggs reported to Walt's office.

About an hour later, he came back, looking several years older, and sagged into an old wicker arm chair, staring at the wall as if lost in deep thought. I was dying to ask him what Walt had said, but I knew if I did I would follow the water bottle out of the window.

In those early years, we had only one woman in the Story Department. Her name was Apalini, and she was of Italian descent.

One morning, Walt killed a story she was working on, and she got terribly upset and went out and bought a bottle of port wine. Locking herself in her room, she drank the whole bottle and got real sick. I had a room next to Suggs', and we both heard her wretching louder than a sick sea lion. We ran to her door and hammered on it. When she wouldn't open it, Suggs broke it open and we took care of her. Our building was the old apartment house and the bathroom was at the end of the hall. Suggs wanted to shove her under the shower or stick her in the tub, but I insisted we wipe her off. What a smelly job!

I never cared much for port wine, but I couldn't stand the stuff after that. Apalini did a fade-out after her big scene, and we never worked near her again.

One Saturday afternoon after work, Suggs told me, in confidence, he intended to get married and wanted my opinion of the apartment he was thinking of renting. I rode with him in his Model T, which he had equipped with two old railroad ties for bumpers. At the stop light, he bumped the car ahead of him, not once, but two or three times. Two Mexicans jumped out in a rage and ran back to confront Suggs, seated calmly behind the wheel grinning at them. After one look at him, they decided to turn the other cheek, and, seeing the light had turned green, jumped into their car and sped away, pronto.

The apartment was in an old brick building in Glendale, and the lady manager, appearing to be somewhat older than the building, showed us around. It had an excellent view from the front windows of Forest Lawn Cemetery, and was a two-bedroom affair. Suggs, following the manager through the rooms, said he didn't like a lot of noise. She assured him her tenants were quiet, and, for the most part, quite elderly. Suggs examined everything minutely, even picking up a heavy, upholstered chair and easily holding it above his head to examine the springs, while the landlady stared at him in amazement. Finally, after I nodded, he agreed to rent the apartment. The manager took in his old shirt with its rolled up sleeves and his wellworn khaki pants (the outfit Suggs always wore) and said she required a deposit. He borrowed a dollar from me and handed it to her. She looked at the silver dollar and back at Suggs, who said that was all he had at the moment, but not to worry as he was a "man of means," and worked for Walt Disney.

We left then, and I glanced back to see her staring down at us from the front window as we jittered away in the Model T, with its two railroad tie bumpers.

The day after renting the apartment, Suggs moved in with his bride and invited us over that same night for a housewarming party. On arriving we had a real surprise, for this wife was not his little mousy fiancee we had expected to see, but a tall, blonde girl with an outgoing personality. He must have made a switch over the weekend.

He laid out big bowls of cold shrimp on the coffee table, and after telling everybody to dig in, he announced he was making Tom Collins. I went into the kitchen to help him.

Glasses lined the sink in a neat row, and I watched as he adroitly rubbed a bit of lime around the rim of each glass, dropped in two ice cubes, and poured in gin like it was water. Then, topping each glass with bubbling Tom Collins mix, said, "Pass 'em out!" In a surprisingly short time, everybody was loaded. The instant a glass was empty, he refilled it. Suggs had an enormous appetite and ate shrimp like salted peanuts, as he judged everybody by himself. The party suddenly got noisy, and the little old lady manager knocked on the door and asked us to please be quiet. Suggs apologized, but one of the girls put a record on the Victrola, and suddenly we all began dancing with the girl closest to us. I had Suggs' new bride, and we did a few fancy steps. She twirled away and fell back into my arms, expecting me to catch her, but I was looking the other way and she fell flat on her face. She glared up at me from the floor. "I've got a notion to sock you!" she said, in a low, menacing voice. But by the time I had helped her up, she had forgotten the incident. Dancing went on, interrupted many times by the building manager, who in desperation finally called the police.

We got out, just ahead of them. Suggs and his bride moved out, too.

At work next morning, I had a hangover and couldn't rid myself of a sickening garlic odor. Reaching into the breast pocket of my jacket for a handkerchief to wipe my perspiring forehead, I pulled out a large neatly folded slice of salami.

Pophoff and I were still working on the bed-building sequence for *Snow White*, on Christmas Eve 1936. At noon, we had had a little studio party just among Story Department employees. Humorous gifts were exchanged, and in mine, I found a small card reading, "Silence Is Golden". It took all the fun out of the party for me. Was it a hint to curb my enthusiasm? Was I getting too big for my britches? All afternoon I was in a depressed mood.

Walt dropped in at quitting time (five o'clock) and went over our sequence until six. He started to leave, then hesitated and said, "Come back to the office." Pophoff and I followed him down the hall worrying about how long this meeting was going to last, because both of us had been invited to Christmas Eve parties. Walt sat down behind his big desk, but we remained standing, a hint we wanted to be off. "Sit down," said Walt. "What's the matter with you?" We took seats facing him, and he continued going over our bed-building sequence. At seven o'clock, he pulled a big checkbook out of his desk and began writing a check. Pophoff and I exchanged winks; a Christmas bonus! No wonder he kept us so late. But he tore out the check, and, folding it neatly, slipped it in his wallet. I could almost hear my hopes hit bottom. He got up and we joined him.

"We'll get back on this after Christmas," he said. We wished him a half-hearted Merry Christmas. He smiled and nodded.

Outside, Pophoff said, "Cheapskate!"

I begged him to give me a ride in his old Ford up to the Hollywood street car line, and he dropped me off there. I missed bus connections and didn't arrive at my party in Westwood until after eleven, and in no mood to enjoy it.

The studio continued to expand, and not long after Christmas, Walt took over another old adjacent apartment building. I was moved into Strayshott and Duddleham's unit. They took over the living room facing out on Hyperion Avenue and relegated me to a small dark room in the rear of the building next to the toilet. Our unit was working on *Beach Picnic*, a Mickey, Donald Duck, and Pluto picture, and I couldn't help wondering if the location of my room had anything to do with the little card I had found in my gift at the Christmas party, because I was on the outer fringe of the unit and never invited to meetings. The vague handwriting on the wall was becoming distinct. One afternoon, the familiar cough sounded in the hallway, and Walt passed my room bound for the toilet. When he came out, he looked in on me. "What are you doing?" he asked. I was hesitant about showing him my idea, since Strayshott and Duddleham had turned it down and had told me to get onto something else. It can't hurt, I thought. At least it will show him I'm trying, so I pulled out a stack of sketches of a sequence with Pluto and a red spotted rubber beach horse. The gentle waves near the beach washed it back and forth around a big rock, and when the waves caused it to make contact with the rock, the air valve on its nose made a sharp "Hiss" sound. Pluto's ears popped up and he splashed out to investigate. The wave had washed the rubber horse out of sight behind the rock, and it bobbed into Pluto's fanny and made a sharp "hiss" sound. The startled dog whirled around, but the wave had washed the horse back out of sight. After several mystifying experiences, the horse came face to face with Pluto. He snarled and bit it on the nose. Then all of the air shot out of the rubber horse into Pluto, swelling him up like a balloon. As the air went out of Pluto, he zoomed around the beach and ended up stuck, fanny-first, in the end of a hollow log.

Walt thought it was a funny piece of business and took my sketches with him to show Strayshott and Duddleham. They thought my sequence was funny, too, and it became a highlight in the completed picture.

I had always liked Pophoff and dropped into his office for a visit one day when he happened to be showing some gags to Walt, who didn't like them and put his dislike in blunt terms. After Walt left the room, Pophoff expressed his feelings by kicking a hole in his storyboard. His foot went through the hole and he couldn't get it out. Just then, Walt looked back in the door and was about to speak when the phone rang. His secretary wanted him, and he left without noticing Pophoff's predicament.

Dill, an assistant animator, came to see me about getting him into the Story Department. I was sure Walt would listen to me if I spoke up for him. He was having a rough time trying to make ends meet, with a sick wife and two kids to support. Perhaps he could do better in the Story Department, and so, during lunch period, I went over to his place with him to see how bad his situation was.

He lived in an old, rundown house. The front door screen had big holes in it, and flies buzzed in and clustered on the ceiling. His wife was in bed, running a fever, and his two kids had colds and their noses, among other things, needed attention.

About one o'clock, I went up to Walt's office to try and get Dill a raise. I went down the long corridor ending in a big glass case, filled with Walt's awards, and turned to his secretary's office. She wasn't back from lunch, and so I walked into his office. He sat hunched over a long coffee table, piled with scripts, and was eating a glazed doughnut. He looked up from the script he was perusing.

"What do you want?" he asked in a friendly way. I said I had come up to talk to him about Dill.

"What about Dill?" he asked. I told him quickly about his condition and ended by saying he was a hard worker and very loyal.

"Loyalty, shit!" Walt exclaimed, and getting up from the table, strode out of the room.

That night I didn't get a nickel's worth of sleep.

Chapter Six

During the last half of 1935 and all of 1936, *Snow White* production was stepped up. Walt was anxious to complete story work on it. Most storymen were shifted from short subjects to *Snow White*. We spent long hours with tireless Walt in story meetings on one sequence after another, thinking up gags.

This is an example:

"MEETING ON SEQUENCE 3B (SNOW WHITE IN THE WOODS), WEDNESDAY, AUGUST 19TH AT 9 A.M. IN MUSIC ROOM #4."

A continuity was delivered to us on the afternoon before meetings so that we could work on gags at home after supper. A variety of gags were desired:

"HOW CAN THE ANIMALS REACT TO THINGS SNOW WHITE SAYS AND BE CUTE ABOUT IT? SNOW WHITE LIES IN THE WOODS FRIGHTENED AFTER ESCAPING FROM THE HUNTER WHO HAS BEEN SENT TO KILL HER. THE ANIMALS HEAR HER SOBBING AND PEEK UP FROM VARIOUS HIDING PLACES."

"WHERE COULD THE ANIMALS BE SO THAT WHEN THEY LOOK UP IT WOULD PRESENT A FUNNY PICTURE?"

"IN WHAT WAY COULD THE ANIMALS RUN OR MOVE THAT MIGHT BE AMUSING?"

"WHAT COULD THE ANIMALS DO TO HELP SNOW WHITE THROUGH THE WOODS?"

"WHAT GAGS CAN YOU SEE OF THE ANIMALS CROSSING THE STREAM?"

Etc., etc.

Meetings requesting gags were endless. In my dreams I worked on gags, and in the morning woke up tired and worried.

The entire studio personnel had to work three nights a week from seven to ten as well as regular hours during the day, plus five hours on Saturday (8 a.m. to 1 p.m.). This extra work was done without extra compensation. Some of the fellows received 50 cents for supper money that benefited the Shack, a half block up the street.

Those suffering most from the big push were the inbetweeners at the bottom of the wage scale, which was rock bottom.

The extreme pressure and close application to their drawing boards caused many of these men to suffer from eye strain and nervous disorders. Due to their poor salaries, many inbetweeners were in hock to doctors.

Pophoff and a sketch man named Tricklebank and I were still assigned to the *Snow White* bed-building sequence. The Dwarfs had decided she was too tall to sleep in one of their beds and set out to find a suitable place to build one for her. Close by their little cottage they found four trees growing in a perfect arrangement to form a bed. The four trunks would serve for four bed posts, and with helpful, jabbered suggestions from their little animal friends, the Dwarfs drew up plans. Everybody set to work with plenty of comedy accidents. Beavers using their sharp teeth planed down logs to form planks. Dopey got his nose stuck in a knothole in one of them. Another Dwarf popped him out of it by bopping him on the nose with a mallet. We created lots of gags and wanted musical spots and were waiting for a meeting with the musician when Snojob dropped in. He said he was also working on a *Snow White* sequence and wanted to see what progress we were making.

Much to Pophoff's discomfort, Snojob went slowly and carefully over our storyboards. Occasionally, he would hesitate, paw his rubbery face as if about to speak, think better of it, assume various expressions; dismay, delight, and profound thought. Finally, twisting his face into an expression of satisfaction, he said, "Good," and left the room.

"Watch out for that guy," Pophoff warned. "He's out for himself."

His remark sent a forgotten incident flashing back through my mind, recalling the days in the Tryout Room when the young redheaded fellow made his remark about Snojob matching quarters with Dogstone and always losing a carton of cigarettes.

About a week later, Sligh dropped in with a sheaf of drawings held together with brass fasteners and given to him by Walt, who thought Snojob had some great stuff and suggested we use his ideas. Pophoff quickly scanned the pages of drawings, his face turning a fiery red.

He let out a yell of rage and dashed out of the room. I picked up the pages of little sketches to see that Snojob had his sketch man duplicate our sequence, combining it with his. I turned to Sligh and said, "The guy stole our stuff!"

"You should have told Walt," cried usually mild-mannered Tricklebank. "Now it looks like we haven't done a damn thing."

Sligh said Walt had dropped the drawings on his desk and left for a meeting before he could examine them.

Sligh eased himself out of the room, and half an hour later Pophoff returned and said Snojob and his sketch man were out (a good thing for Snojob), but he had let him know what he thought of him by emptying out his desk drawers, tearing up every scrap of work he could find, and scattering it all over the room. It wasn't good to cross Pophoff.

Neither Tricklebank nor I had cars and paid Snojob to ride back and forth to work in his old black-and red-trimmed touring car.

On our way home that night, Snojob said he'd heard we were upset with him. "What did I do wrong?" he said.

"You swiped our bed-building sequence," cried Tricklebank.

Snojob shook his head. "Oh no, you guys are wrong. I wanted to make a nice flow of the two sequences."

"You did it alright," said Tricklebank, whom I'd never seen mad before. "You flowed our work right into Walt. You stole our sequence and don't deny it."

Turning to me, Snojob said, "What do you think?"

"It wasn't cricket," I said.

And that ended our rides with Snojob. Not long afterwards, Walt found *Snow White* was running too long, and, as very little animation had been done on the bed-building sequence, shelved it.

Chapter Seven

Snow White was completed, and, on the evening of December 21, 1937, was given a world premiere at the Carthay Circle Theater in Los Angeles. The following paragraph appeared on the program:

> My sincere appreciation to members of my staff whose loyalty and creative endeavor made possible this production.
>
> Walt Disney

Snow White was a tremendous success and was released all over America and in Europe.

None of us knew the extent of Walt and his brother Roy's financial success, but that little paragraph on the program made us feel we would no longer be laboring for substandard wages. Now we, too, would soon share in the success of *Snow White*.

But months went by and nothing happened. Walt kept us too busy to brood for long. He was starting work on two new features, Carlo Collodi's *Pinocchio* (the tale of a little wooden puppet) and Felix Salten's *Bambi* (the story of a deer). Walt had also scheduled eleven short subjects for 1938. All talk was about future production, nothing about the past. Just the mention of *Snow White* brought a scowl to his face. *Snow White* was already behind him, and he was charging ahead with new projects. His walk had changed, too.

He leaned forward more, as if striding into a brisk wind, as if he couldn't get to where he was going fast enough. Walt drove onward, never looking into the rear-view mirror of life.

He dropped the past from his shoulders like an old cloak, a cloak that had our salary increases in the lining.

We began to think those warm words of praise on the *Snow White* program were hollow words designed to impress the public, when we had a surprise. Walt suddenly announced a party for his staff on

Saturday, June 4, 1938. It was to be held at the no-longer-used Lake Narconian Country Club, in Corona, a town nestling in a corner of the Pomona Valley about 40 miles east of Los Angeles.

The party was planned to last 24 hours, and all the food and lodging was free. A program was sent to all employees containing a list of games and sporting events. On the cover, lettered in green ink, was:

WALT'S FIELD DAY...1938[13]

Below this was a drawing of Mickey Mouse wearing a happy smile and getting set to drive a golf ball down the fairway. Inside the cover was a dedication:

BELIEVE IT OR NOT, THIS IS A DAY DEDICATED TO THE FORGETTING OF SWEATBOXES, ANIMATION FOOTAGE AND CELLULOIDS. IT IS MY SINCERE WISH THAT YOU ENJOY YOURSELF TO THE UTMOST, AND THAT YOU WILL FIND THE DAY ONE OF COMPLETE PLEASURE AND RELAXATION.
WALT

Saturday, the day of the party, turned out to be one of those hotter-than-hell days for which Corona was noted. The swimming pool was full and so were a lot of the staff by evening. There was no air conditioning, and by the time Sligh was about to hand out awards for the various events, the dance floor was at baking temperature. Worn out, soaked in sweat and sunburned, we waited in happy anticipation, for we knew Walt would make a big announcement this night.

Walt was a showman waiting for the perfect moment to step forward and announce the amount of money to compensate each man. What other reason could there be for the big party?

At last he walked onto the stage. Deafening applause greeted him. Here it was! The good news we had waited so long to hear.

But Walt made a long speech all about production having fallen way off. He hoped his party would inspire us all to greater efforts.

He left to a sliver of the applause that had greeted him.

"One big blow-out for all those years of hard work. That was our reward," said old Jiggins.

Friends gathered to hash over Walt's speech. Could the party have been given in lieu of extra money? Could Jiggins have been right? Walt was a peculiar guy. You couldn't tell what he would do next. Maybe he was going to hand us a real surprise, and he did. A little over three weeks later, on Tuesday, June 28, 1938, the following exciting news appeared in the *Los Angeles Examiner*:

DISNEY TO GIVE STAFF 20 PCT OF PROFIT ON SNOW WHITE
Distribution of 20 per cent of the earnings from the motion picture *Snow White and the Seven Dwarfs* to Walt Disney's employees was announced today.

The distribution to employees will be between $800,000 and $1,000,000, with the division being made on a salary basis. It is estimated that the bonus to each employee will represent about 12 to 13 weeks' wages.

About 800 workers will share in the bonus.

Little did we know at the time that *Snow White*, by 1967, would have grossed well over $27,000,000. But that article in the *Examiner* raised morale a hundred percent. On the strength of the promised bonus, men bought new cars and household appliances, and signed contracts to buy new houses. One divorced wife went to court and had her alimony increased.

Walt was the greatest guy on earth. Now we definitely would be compensated for those long hours of hard work at sweatshop wages.

Walt and his brother Roy were well on the way to becoming millionaires, and we would share in their good fortunes.

The morning after the good news, several of us went up to Jiggins' office. He was seated in his ancient, greasy, upholstered chair, the top of his white head showing over his newspaper.

We reminded him of his cynical remark at the party.

"What do you say now, Jiggins?" we asked, and waited for his answer. Jiggins carried a lot of weight with the fellows around the studio. He was a old-timer in the animated cartoon game, dating back to the early days; besides, he had invented a process that had revolutionized animated cartoons.

Jiggins lowered his paper and dusted the cigarette ashes off the front of the button-up sweater he wore winter and summer.

"Anybody for tennis?" he said, grinning.

Jiggins was sore at Walt, we thought, and we couldn't blame him. Walt rode him all the time and criticized his work, even though Jiggins came up every now and then with terrific ideas, like the first speed gag. We guessed Walt was griped because he might have had to pay Jiggins a royalty on his invention.[14]

Time passed with no further mention of a bonus. Studio management never confirmed the *Examiner* story, but more important to us, they never denied it, either.

About this time, Walt made more plans for the future. He started a training program offering unlimited opportunities to new artists.

A booklet of 31 pages was printed, illustrated with pencil drawings of studio characters, including Snow White and the Dwarfs, and entitled *An Introduction to THE WALT DISNEY STUDIOS*, describing the various departments requiring artists. If accepted after a four-week tryout period, an artist could expect a starting salary of between $18 and $30 a week. In the Animation Department alone, there was a possibility of 100 positions a year being offered.

The booklet also mentioned that, although television was in its infancy, the future offered vast opportunities for the studio, because tests had proven nothing could equal the clarity of Walt's cartoons.

Dogstone, the head of the Inbetween Department, was dispatched to New York to interview and test applicants.[15]

Since then, I've often asked myself the motives for this training program—developing new talent or building an oversupply of talent to keep wages low?

Months passed and the bonus had not been paid, but we didn't worry, we were sure the accounting department was busy figuring out the amount of money due each employee on the basis of 20 weeks' salary, and that took time.

Then we had an unpleasant surprise. Walt had purchased a 51-acre tract in Burbank and planned to build a large studio on it.

The studio was to be plush and air-conditioned, designed for years ahead.

Pictures of Walt appeared in magazines, showing him seated on the floor of his office, poring over blue prints.

I think that was the beginning of hard feelings between the staff and Walt, but a lot of the fellows thought the bonus was bound to be paid, otherwise Walt never would have published an account of his intentions in a newspaper.

During the long period of great expectations, Suggs bought a long narrow lot in the suburbs with a small tract-type house plunked down on the street end of it. The house had one tiny bathroom and Suggs, always the gag-man, put in a twenty-watt red globe and dangled toy spiders from the ceiling on wires, creating a scary effect so women guests "wouldn't hang in there too long, gossiping".

Working weekends, he enclosed the yard with a high wooden fence, even plugging the knothole to frustrate any peeping toms.

Gradually, he added other features such as a brick barbeque area that he thatched over with palm fronds to give the appearance of a Tahitian hut. Suggs, never a man to do things in a small way, also built a sprinkler system and installed it on the roof so he could have a tropical downpour at will. And he added thunder by means of a sheet tin contraption which he would rattle convincingly as he created lightning by switching lights on and off rapidly.

But he wasn't through yet. He put in a small swimming pool, unheated, to keep guests from soaking in it.

And on the back of his little garage, he built a dressing room with a thatched roof about the size of two broom closets. On one door was lettered GENTS and on the other, DAMES. After entering their respective doors, they faced each other in one tiny room. Suggs had neglected to install a dividing wall, but had thoughtfully painted a broad white stripe as a dividing line.

Suggs had a green thumb, too, and stuffed his narrow lot with bushes, flowers, trees, and vegetable plants, until going from one place to another was like running an obstacle course. But when you went over to his place, you were sure to have a surprise.

While the new studio was in the planning stage, Walt's increased production schedule forced him to build an annex across the street from the main building and also acquire two old apartment houses next door to each other and adjacent to the parking lot. Nevertheless, these two extra facilities could barely accommodate the increased Short Cartoons Department and the new *Pinocchio* unit. More space had to be found for the *Bambi* unit, and so an abandoned building was leased in Hollywood, some 20 miles from the old Hyperion plant. Work on renovating the building had hardly begun, when, to my dismay, I was transferred to the *Bambi* unit. It seemed I was always being moved farther away from the main stream. And my mental elevator hit bottom when I discovered Snojob was in charge of production. Then, I knew that whenever he looked at me, he would be reminded of the *Snow White* bed-building sequence and that he had been a gag stealer.

When I reported to the *Bambi* unit, Snojob saw to it that I had a room about the size of a coat closet, with a small, dirty window, and located right in the middle of the sawing and hammering activity. He was too busy to see me, so sent a traffic boy around with model sheets of the characters and instructions to start thinking up spot gags.

The next day, Longshanks arrived and was assigned to a similar room next to mine. I don't know what Snojob had against him.

We had not been there four weeks before we were both sent back to Hyperion, as not being suited for work on *Bambi*. My spirits hit the sub-basement. Snojob had buried the knife to the hilt, and now I would be "pink slipped".

I was called up to see the number two man in the studio, a big handsome fellow. He set me at ease when he said, "Don't worry, Homer. We like you," and gave me a raise.

Longshanks and I were back on short subjects again, and glad of it. Some months later, "Number Two" had to take over the *Bambi* unit and complete the production. For a while Snojob was at loose ends, but he had Walt's ear and became connected with a live-action feature based on the book *Midnight and Jeremiah*, by Sterling North. It became *So Dear to My Heart*, but Walt's brother-in-law referred to it as "So Dear to My Pocketbook", because it was running way over budget.

A couple of years later Longshanks walked out and surfaced afterward as Disney's comic book publisher.

The new studio was completed, and I was assigned to the second floor, "G" wing, room #1. I shared this room with Monks, a tall, raw-boned, moody fellow, one of the younger animators who had requested a transfer to the Story Department.

Our room was spacious, carpeted in dark blue and with two new desks and high, chrome-legged stools with blue naugahyde seats. Our storyboards covered the walls, and several comfortable lounging chairs faced them.

We had been accustomed to uncarpeted floors and peeling walls and felt out of place in these bright new rooms.

I said, "Take your pick of the desks."

"I'll take this one," he said, "so I can have my back to the wall. It's there anyway."

Monks' story was a haunted castle tale, with Mickey and Minnie.

Mine was *The Fire Chief*, with a cast of Donald Duck and his three nephews, Huey, Louey, and Duey.

Monks read the morning paper while I threw a few push-pins into a storyboard by way of warming up. The silence was broken by the sound of a distant cough. "Walt," whispered Monks, and crumpled his newspaper into the waste basket. I was busily sketching when Walt strode into the room and slumped into a chair facing Monk's boards. This was one of his surprise visits. You never could tell when he might pop in.

Although Monks knew Walt well, this was his first story meeting, and he suffered from stage fright. His color changed like a chameleon's, and he started telling his story in a hesitant manner. Instantly reminded of Strayshott's slow style, I said to myself "For God's sake, faster!" Soon, Walt was drumming on the arm of his chair, and I had learned that when he did that you wished you'd stayed in bed.

Walt lit a cigarette and took a long inhale, followed by a hollow cough. The tattoo on the arm of the chair continued unabated while Monks explained his story, letting out nervous giggles at his favorite gags. Walt remained silent all through the story, and when Monks finished, the only sound was Walt's fingers drumming steadily on the arm of that damned chair.

Monks and I exchanged glances; sweat beaded his forehead. He finally broke the silence. "H-How did you like it, Walt?"

Walt, never one to spare anyone's feelings, said, "Maybe you should have stayed in animation."

Walt seemed unnecessarily cruel. Monks didn't deserve this. He had been in the studio a long time and was the picture of misery as Walt abruptly swung his chair around to face my boards. "Let's see what you've got," he said. I felt like crawling under the carpet. Now it was my turn to sweat, for Monks' story was far better drawn than mine. I took the pointer and began explaining it. When I ran through a story, I got excited, forgot my audience, and lived it. I was unaware that Pophoff, Longshanks, and Belter, along with a secretary, had slipped into the room. The girl had busily set up her stenotype machine and was recording a verbatim transcript.

I played up the Duck's pompous manner as he waved away his nephew's efforts to get his attention. He ordered full pressure on the hose, ignoring the kids, who tried to tell him there was a knot in it. While he glared at the trickle of water coming from the nozzle, a tremendous bulge in the hose was building up behind him, growing to the size of a big building.

Donald shouted angrily, "Let me have it!", just as the hose burst and he was carried away on a roaring river. He shot across the street and through a green house and a sporting goods store. He zoomed out of the back door astride a bike, and, slamming on the brakes, ground the bike down to a pile of dust. Then, running back to his fire truck, he saw the fire was in his own station. He jerked the new hose out of his nephews' hands, and, looking back over his shoulder at the fire, accidentally screwed the hose onto the gas tank of his truck instead of the fire hydrant, located right next to it. He squirted gasoline onto his burning fire house. In seconds all that remained was a black-ribbed skeleton, and it collapsed into a head of ashes with a "poof" sound. The action was continuous and the gasoline, traveling back in the hose, consumed the fire truck in seconds, leaving a skeleton. It collapsed with the same "poof" as as the fire house. To top the sequence, Donald's fire chief's hat went up the same way, leaving a blackened skeleton, and it collapsed with a "poof" into a small heap of ashes on his head. The three "poofs" in rapid succession were funny, and the story ended with the Duck doing a terrific "burn" at the audience.

Here are a few reactions taken down by the secretary:

WALT: I think it's swell. It's a natural. It's sort of like Homer, isn't it. It has Homer's pep and enthusiasm to it. This is a good one. It has a lot of good surprises in it.

POPHOFF: What we need now, is some time to catch up with the animation director. He is going like hell and this will catch up time. We might as well move this in, Walt.

WALT: There's some good, funny stuff in there, guys.

POPHOFF: Yes, it's funny; it's a good little picture.

Walt referred to a fire truck extension ladder gag. The Duck had pressed a button and the ladder shot him high in the air.

WALT: That ladder thing seems funny. It could build a little more there.

HOMER: He goes through a cloud.

WALT: Goes through a cloud before he realizes he's up there, and he goes through the cloud and looks around. Where the hell is he?

Fire Chief was given a production number and moved at once into the Director's Unit, where Pophoff, Longshanks, and Belter would tighten it up for Layout and Animation.

Seventeen days later, a final meeting was held in the Director's Unit; the picture was ready for production. Walt sat in on the meeting, but I had not been invited. Afterwards, I asked the recording secretary for a copy of the meeting notes. Now we see what happened.

Longshanks reviewed the continuity.

WALT: Seems like this is more complicated than it was before.

LONGSHANKS: In Homer's stuff there were a lot of places where there was a lot of business, but there was really no gag there—just a lot of running around—and we were trying to eliminate the running around parts, and that's how we happened to get a lot of new stuff.

WALT: Well, a lot of that stuff is kind of old. There were some things in Homer's stuff that were newer. I thought the ladder was a funny thing. And I don't like this beginning as well as the one Homer had.

The discussion went on and Walt asked to see my storyboards. They were brought in.

WALT: It seems like this opening is funnier. They fire up the boiler; it seems like it's funnier to me. I like Homer's development.

The meeting was long and involved, as the three tried to hang on to their changes, but Walt ordered the story to be put back in the same form it was when I delivered it to them.

A call from Walt came after lunch. He suggested Monks and I work as a team. He thought Monks would develop into a good sketch man, and, working together, we could turn out stories faster.

Monks' ghost story was shelved, and that year the two of us did a number of stories in collaboration and concluded with a remake of an old Pluto sequence. The story, retitled *Lend a Paw*, won an Academy Award for Walt as the best short cartoon for 1941.

Chapter Eight

I believe it was in the spring of 1940 when Walt began wearing colorful matching outfits. I remember a couple; one was a burgundy slack suit of light material, loose jacket, slacks, and matching pork pie hat with matching shoes. I remember a yellow outfit, too. I think he wanted to create a new image. New studio, new clothes. Walt had always worn sport clothes, but nothing like these outfits. The mood of his employees didn't match his, and he must have realized this, because he soon resumed his former attire.

Monks and I were requested to attend a meeting on a cartoon feature, *Jack and the Beanstalk*. The storyman, Bigger, reviewed the continuity, and when he finished Walt's first remark was, "This is a good example of how we don't want to do it."[16]

Bigger left the studio of his own volition shortly after the meeting, saying Walt and he had agreed to disagree.

Before the meeting, Bigger occupied a room across the hall from Monks and me. He was a thickset man, very secretive, and always worked with his door closed.

After the meeting, his storyboards were turned over to us, and we moved into larger quarters on the second floor. Our help consisted of two sketch men.

By late May, a deep dissatisfaction developed among the employees. The new studio was being considered a wretched place to work. Word got round through the grapevine, and Walt issued the following stern inter-office communication on his green stationery:

SPECIAL NOTICE TO ALL EMPLOYEES

An emergency exists. Each production hour of everybody in the plant is very valuable and if our time is properly spent and utilized, it may mean that some worthwhile person will be able to retain his job.

I am calling on everybody to help me. We will have to work for the utmost in economy in the use of our time and see to it that every hour of the day is well spent.

I do not want to deny people their privileges. On the contrary, we are trying to design a plan whereby everyone will be able to continue to enjoy the privileges now in effect. By this, I mean the Coffee Shop, the recreation facilities and the noontime showings in the theatre.

However, there has been a terrific loss of time, due to certain people taking uncalled-for advantages. Rather than cut off these things, I feel that if I draw these matters to your attention, you will cooperate with me.

First on the list is the business of getting down to work on time.

Also, there must be less time spent away from the studio on your own business. Why not let your wife or someone else handle these things for you so that you will be making every working hour count.

All of those people who have been engaged in other pursuits during the lunch period and then eat their lunch on the company's time must take notice.

It has been brought to my attention that there are those who engage in such vigorous games throughout the noon hour that it is necessary for them to take a goodly part of the afternoon to calm and rest themselves before they are able to pick up with their work. In the future it will be necessary that all such violent exercise be taken after hours.

There are those restless people who go through rooms and bore those who are working with their idle, useless chatter. All such visiting must cease.

The wanton waste of supplies must be curtailed. In the future, each and every person in the studio will be held accountable for the supplies given them.

For those of you who, in the past, found it necessary to sleep on the company's time—due to lack of sleep the night before—it is strongly recommended that you get the proper amount of rest before coming to work.

I trust that it will not be necessary for me to take the drastic steps that have been suggested to me and I feel confident that once you have been made aware of the existing conditions, I can depend on you to give me your whole-hearted cooperation.

June 8, 1940

WALT

Walt's special notice was like tossing bullets on a smoldering fire. Explosive criticism almost blew the studio apart. Walt was called "a double-crossing S.O.B." Many fellows were outspoken, but the majority heeded Walt's admonitions and went along with him. The executives, "the double-breasted boys" as we called them, because they wore dark, double-breasted suits, circulated among us, soothing us, blaming the loss of foreign markets on the war. True, the loss of the European markets hurt Walt's pocket book, but that had nothing to do with the *Snow White* bonus promised back in 1938. And that bonus was the root of the resentment. Walt had gone out on a limb, financially, and the limb had been chopped off. Fellows compared Walt to the grasshopper in his Silly Symphony, *The Grasshopper and the Ants*. He had fiddled away the profits on *Snow White* and had not prepared for a rainy day. But, unlike the grasshopper, Walt was not humble; he never blamed himself for failures. He blamed his employees - they worked too slow to meet the emergencies he created.

The new, immaculate fantasy factory in Burbank boiled with turmoil, unheard of in the old Hyperion days. Workers were at odds with each other. Long-time studio friendships broke up. Secretaries took sides. The *Jack and the Beanstalk* feature was shelved. Directors needed shorts to keep their animation crews working, and, under heavy pressure, the Story Department turned out *Mickey's Birthday Party, Bell Boy Donald*, and *Donald's Show Fight*. Walt began dropping into my room. Once I mentioned joining an evening art class to improve my drawing. "Forget it," he said. "What I need are idea men. Artists are a dime a dozen!"

He was right. I believe about fifty percent of the studio artists made less than $50 a week.

My two weeks of vacation was scheduled in July. I was so nervous from overwork that I spent the first week trembling and the second week trying to stop trembling.

On October 24, 1940, the Wage and Hour Law went into effect. Walt felt the government had struck him another blow. Now he had to pay time-and-a-half for night and Saturday work. His brother Roy was forced to notify all personnel:

Beginning Monday, October 28th, 1940, certain changes in the allowed number of working hours become effective in accordance with the Wage Hour Law.

The studio will remain open as usual from 8:30 A.M. to 5:30 P.M., Monday thru Friday, and 8:30 A.M. to 12:30 P.M. on Saturday.

New regulations have made it necessary to reclassify various groups in the studio and those people whose classification has changed will be notified by individual memorandum.

It will be the policy of the studio to conform in every way with the provisions of the Wage Hour Law and overtime will be paid to all those non-exempt employees required to work more than 40 hours per week.

Naturally, the reduction in working hours will add a further burden of overtime payments to the losses already suffered through the curtailment of foreign revenues. May we urge you to consider those facts and to recognize the necessity for maintaining the heavy production schedule upon which we have embarked.

For the first time in five-and-a-half years I would receive overtime! I was elated. But any pleasure I got from the new law was spoiled by the usual rumor of Christmas layoffs. Ever since *Snow White* had been released, mysterious reports of Christmas layoffs circulated through the studio prior to the holidays. The reports were never denied, simply dismissed by the "double-breasted" boys with a knowing wink, a grin, or a shrug of the shoulders. I believe Walt thought that by giving the employees a feeling of insecurity they would work faster.

And, looking back on it, this philosophy surprises me. Walt was terrific at working with men and getting the maximum out of them. Surely he would know that, while some men worked best with a deadline, others planned their work so well that no extra spurring was needed. By the same token, some workers needed to be constantly shaken up, and others worked best in an atmosphere of peace and serenity. Why Walt continued to work on the premise that we all needed to feel insecure was a mystery to me.

We weathered another jittery Christmas, and our low spirits were not improved when, on February 6, 1941, all employees received the following communication from Walt:

URGENT!

Statistics prove that the footage output of the plant for the past six weeks has dropped 50%. It is obvious that a great deal of valuable studio time is being consumed in discussing union matters that should be taken care of on free time.

The Company recognizes the right of employees to organize and join in any labor organization of their own choosing, and the Company does not intend to interfere in this right. HOWEVER, the law clearly provides that matters of this sort should be done off the employer's premises and on the employees own time, and in such a manner as not to interfere with production.

Due to world conditions, the studio is facing a crisis about which a lot of you are evidently unaware. It can be solved by your undivided attention to production matters. This is an appeal to your sense of fairness and I trust it will be sufficient to remedy the matter.

Sincerely,

Walt

P.S. A copy of this memorandum is being filed with the N.L.R.B. (the National Labor Relations Board).

Walt

This appeal to our "sense of fairness", coming from the man who had reneged on his promise to pay us twenty percent of his profits from *Snow White*, created an angry, resentful mood instead of the speed-up in production.

Monks and I had finished story work on *Lend a Paw*, and we were casting around for another idea when Walt ordered us to split up. There was no reason for it. We were a successful combination, but there was no appeal from Walt's decision.

This was another abnormality of his. It had happened before and it would happen again. Whenever a team of storymen clicked, Walt invariably moved in and separated them. I never could understand his strange behavior. Perhaps he didn't want anybody in the Story Department to feel too secure.

Walt later used an analogy of his being a bee and buzzing around the studio mixing up pollen. He certainly mixed up the Story Department. Perhaps he felt that one or two successes would give the story teams swelled heads. Maybe he thought that a success would lead to coasting and not putting out 100% effort. But, that goes back to his basic ideas about people.

Should they be treated as individuals and allowed to take pride in their accomplishments? Or, as mass workers, needing constant prodding.

Walt was a perfectionist. Maybe he believed sincerely that no matter how good a story team was, he could scramble them around and find a better one. Could be that's why he did it.

Monks took the break-up hard. He couldn't work by himself, and he wouldn't go back to animation, so he left the studio.

I was moved up to the top floor to begin work on a new short subject. At that time, an animation director was making a *How To Do It* series starring Goofy. He insisted on working out the stories himself and directing them, but when he came up with a couple of turkeys, Walt cast around for fresh ideas. He ordered me to think up a story using Goofy, and I suggested, *How to Be a Sailor*. Walt gave me the green light and I went into preliminary work. Concentration was hard, for studio personnel had been split like a tree hit by lightning. Production continued to fall off. Those of us still loyal to Walt held night meetings discussing plans for a union of our own. Sometimes these meetings on both sides carried over into working hours, and the following terse inter-office communication was circulated throughout the studio by Walt's brother Roy. It was dated July 24, 1941:

"Any discussion of union activities or infraction of established company rules on company property during working hours will be considered cause for immediate dismissal."

Walt labeled the group calling for a strike "the radicals". This group felt no satisfying results could be obtained by forming what they termed a "company union".

Suddenly, a labor leader, Herb Sorrell, backed them. His advice gave this group renewed confidence. And Walt sent two of his trusted management lieutenants on a scouting expedition throughout the studio to report to him any information they could glean and also report any infractions of working rules. Whenever those two men, Smirks and Wetmore, came into our rooms, we "clammed up". Wetmore had started in the studio as a traffic boy and used to ask my opinion of gags he wanted to submit in order to make a little extra money. Later, he worked his way into the management end. Smirks came to the studio in a vague position. Both men felt secure in their positions. They knew Walt always took better care of his management teams than he did of his creative personnel.

Resentment among the creative staff had built until the dam was full and overflowing. What happened next would be a bitter memory for Walt.

Chapter Nine

The dam broke in the summer of 1941 and engulfed the studio in one of the most bitter strikes in the history of Hollywood.

In those hot, dry summer months, Walt's dream factory produced nightmares. The strikers saw themselves as an army of slaves, rising without a Spartacus to lead them, and turning against a despot who may have tried to be benevolent but was merely a miser. To Disney, the strike represented the sons rebelling against the father-figure, and Walt's family bickered, snarled, snapped, and fought, tearing itself asunder.

From that day on, employees would never have the fraternal feeling of the old days.

Walt blamed the strike, as he once told me, on the "goddamned Communists". But it wasn't primarily the Communists. It was Walt himself. The strike was pure and simple an explosion of long frustrations.

Driving to work one morning, I was confronted by pickets marching in a circle in front of the main gate on Buena Vista Avenue. They carried signs reading: "On Strike", "Disney Unfair", "Sweat Shop", etc., etc. I started to drive through the gates, but they stopped my car, and, hopping on the running board, begged me to join them. I knew all the fellows, but we were in separate camps long before the strike, and I refused to join them, for I was strongly of the opinion they were wrong.

So I drove inside the gates to a chorus of "boos" ringing in my ears.

Walt arrived to hear himself called a lot of unkind names. One striker called him a "goddamned blood sucker". Walt had a short temper. He skidded his car to a stop inside the gates, leaped out, and ran back to face his tormentor. The striker met him, fists doubled, ready to fight. Walt changed his mind, went back inside, and the gates slammed shut. A striker yelled after him, "We'll turn your sweat shop into a hospital. That's what it was designed for!"

Another shouted, "You'll never get any more animation done in this dump."

Walt laughed and called back over his shoulder that he had a vault full of pictures. Where would the strikers be?

"Not starving to death trying to make a buck out of you!" they shouted.

Walt turned on his heel and gave a nasty laugh.

I had been standing near the gate listening. After the confrontation, Walt strode toward the main building, leaning forward as if driving into a heavy wind.

He was in a helluva temper when I was called into his office for a story meeting. His secretary silently served orange juice, doughnuts, and coffee. Walt sat moodily consuming a couple of doughnuts while we watched apprehensively. Suddenly, he jumped to his feet and shouted, "I'll shut the goddamned studio down! I'll pull the chain! It's time I flushed the joint!" His tirade muted the meeting, for he had lumped his loyal workers with the strikers! For the life of me I couldn't come up with anything funny that morning, and I spent the rest of the day worrying about passing through the picket lines at 5:30 that evening.

When we drove home the strikers urged us to join them. They shouted, "Don't rat on your friends. Herb Sorell's behind us! Herb says if we stick together we'll get a fair shake." I drove home that night with their parting shots ringing in my ears. "How did you like your *Snow White* bonus?"

Next morning Walt declared, "Not one of those sonsofbitches will ever work for me again!"

It wasn't until after the strike had been settled that I found my loyalty to Walt had been all one-sided.

A striking assistant animator used to jump on the running board of my car and call me a "dirty, rotten scab" when I tried to drive through the studio gates. Later, the guy became one of Walt's management team!

The headquarters for the strike was the field across the street from the studio, where St. Joseph's Hospital now is.

There was a little raised hill with a dirt path leading up to it and big eucalyptus trees all around. The strikers set up a tent town and had a kitchen operation there to serve food.

I heard it was awful, but it was one way of getting something to eat.

A line of old cars going up the hill looked like something out of *The Grapes of Wrath*.

Certain men were assigned to pick up the meeting area during the strike and went around picking up scraps of paper. If nothing else, the strikers were neat.

As the strike wore on, finance companies repossessed cars and some men lost their homes, yet they stayed on strike, encouraged by Herb Sorell's promises. Loud speakers were set up and one of the strike leaders, an important union official, addressed us one morning as we came to work. "Wake up, get wise, you guys," he shouted. "Disney will squeeze the last drop of blood out of you and toss you aside. This is labor's day! Join your friends and we'll have power, and power is all that guy Disney respects!" These may not be his exact words, but they were the gist of what he said, and when none of the loyal employees heeded him, he said he would show us what he meant by power.

I never saw the gasoline circle, mentioned many times, but the union boss did have a huge parade in front of the main gate, and police had to be called in to maintain order.

The morning following the parade, the *Los Angeles Times* published a couple of pages of pictures of the parading strikers. While I was studying them, Walt came into my room, and, taking a magnifying glass, examined the pictures, and then, grabbing a grease pencil, circled faces of strikers he recognized. Many of the paraders were strangers, and Walt said, "They've imported a lot of goons." Then, folding my paper, he took it with him and left the room.

The speeches continued over the loud speakers, and pleadings and threatening shouts were directed at us morning and night. One night my house was "egged".

Late in the summer, the strikers had become a pathetic sight. Single men who could no longer pay rent were allowed to live in the tent headquarters. They cooked frugal meals over camp fires, washed their clothes, and hung them to dry on lines strung between trees.

Then, to our dismay, we learned Walt was trying to shut the studio down, but, since no official union existed, he was unable to do it. Closing the studio would have been called a lock-out by the Labor Board.

A few years later, I met a Labor Board executive at a cocktail party. He was a high-ranking member of the Board in Los Angeles during the time Walt was fighting the unionization of his studio. He told me that Walt used to come to his office and, with tears in his eyes, tell of how his employees had taken advantage of his kindness to them. I doubted his story because I couldn't imagine Walt in tears.

As the strike dragged on, we loyal employees decided to go ahead and form our own union, unaware that Walt had been making secret plans which would have a profound effect on us.

In order to hold an election of officers, we rented the Burbank American Legion Hall for $50. It was located on the top floor of a two-story building on Olive Street. June bugs stayed late that year, and, drawn by the light, flew in through open windows, thudding against the walls.

Sligh and Strayshott took turns addressing us from the little stage. We cheered them while some of the strikers, who had sneaked in, booed loudly. Sligh, in his quiet, unemotional way, reminded us that Walt was counting on our loyalty to him. But it was a character designer who gave the star performance.

The little former polo player, with social background, money, and a wealth of self-confidence, made a stirring speech and was unanimously nominated for president of our union. The charter, etc., would be drawn up later. He was effusive in his thanks, but wanted someone else to be president and promised to work hard on our behalf.

Next morning came a shattering surprise: Walt, our new mentor, the polo player, Sligh, Strayshot, and thirteen other studio employees had left by plane for a three-month goodwill tour of South America.[17] Security in the studio had really been tight. Not a word of the trip, nor the people chosen to take it with Walt, had leaked out. The captain and a picked crew had deserted the ship. Unknown to us, the government had requested that Walt make a trip to South America as a goodwill ambassador.

I knew that one doesn't simply pick up and fly to South America in a few hours. Passports in those war days took weeks to obtain, and there were typhoid shots and vaccinations. All those men had to know about the trip several months in advance. The dirty part of it was that all of them at the meeting that night knew they were going to desert us.

When Roy Disney was assured Walt and his party were safely on their way, he immediately sent out the following sad news:

NOTICE TO ALL EMPLOYEES

The Board of Directors of Walt Disney Productions has today found it necessary to order the temporary suspension of general operations of its plant until September 2, 1941, commencing as of the close of business today and to lay off all personnel without pay excepting those necessary to perform essential maintenance work and the completion of certain emergency commitments. Employees necessary for such services have been separately notified.

All employees are requested to appear for work on September 2, 1941, unless previously notified by mail of a different date. All employees working through tonight will be paid up to Monday night (August 18th). Checks for pay to Monday night may be picked up at the Buena Vista gate at 3:30 P.M. Monday. Checks not picked up by 5:30 P.M. will be mailed to the employees Monday night.

The management will not be responsible for any personal effects left in the studio during the time the operations are suspended.

By the order of The Board of Directors of WALT DISNEY PRODUCTIONS

August 15, 1941

Now all of Walt's loyal workers were kicked out. None us knew whether or not the studio would ever reopen. The feeling that it wouldn't was heightened by the last paragraph in the notice, stating they would not be responsible for personal effects left in the studio.

We loaded up our briefcases with our possessions. Then we had to go through a humiliating experience. Smirks ordered us to line up in single file near the front gate like prisoners being checked through a security guard. A studio policeman stood next to Smirks, who, wearing a Cheshire Cat grin, stopped each of us as we passed before him and made a minute examination of our effects. He dug deep into briefcases and confiscated pencils, erasers, sheets of paper, and books. They would be returned to us if found not to be part of the studio's library. As Smirks checked us out, the pile of material beside him grew, and the strikers watching outside the gate enjoyed the humiliation of the "loyalists".

As we drove homeward through the main gate, they jeered and they put their hearts into it. At last the "kiss-ass boys" had been booted out.

I drove home in a state of shock, for I had a wife and child to support. Now I knew how the strikers felt. I consoled myself by thinking about my contract. Suppose the studio didn't reopen, where would

I find work? Doctors, lawyers, accountants, carpenters, plumbers could find work in any city, but where would I find another position offering the kind of specialized work I had been engaged in? Cartoon studios were few and far between. Walt's training program had flooded the Hollywood market.

The following day I received a letter from the studio written the day the studio shut down. The letter was in respect to my contract and the second paragraph advised me as follows:

"Pursuant to paragraph 17 of your agreement of employment, we have elected to and hereby do suspend the operation of said agreement for said two weeks period."

That was my reward, along with a flock of enemies over at the striker's camp, for my loyalty to Walt.

In those confusing minutes after reading the letter, I remembered what Walt had said to me when I had tried to get a salary increase for Dill, and recalled reading somewhere that great leaders who could inspire loyalty in their workers seldom had any loyalty themselves.

On August 27, 1941, a telegram came from the studio informing me that I would lose a month's salary instead of the two weeks previously announced. The studio would reopen September 15, "UNLESS OTHERWISE NOTIFIED...".

Chapter Ten

The strike ended on September 15, 1941, and the studio reopened. All strikers had been reinstated, but there was deep bitterness toward the loyal employees and friction again developed in the "fantasy factory".

The chief agitator during the strike was one of the best animators.[18] After the strike was over, he came back, but not a single director in the studio could find work for him to do, and he sat around doing nothing. Finally, he was laid off or quit, and filed suit against the studio.

I heard fault was found with the work of the principal "trouble makers", and they were gradually weeded out on grounds of inefficiency.

Walt and his South American tour group returned after the strike, having been fortunate in avoiding the hard times. They opened a unit on the third floor and struggled to turn their experiences into a series of short cartoons to be tied together later with 16-millimeter, live-action footage shot on visits to Bolivia, Chile, Argentina, and Brazil. The finished product was to be released as a short feature entitled *Saludos Amigos*.

I had returned to work on my short subject, *How to Be a Sailor*. It was a story of Goofy in the Navy during the war. After learning the ropes, he became a crewman on a sub, and, in launching a torpedo, accidentally went into the tube along with the torpedo. Clinging to it, he rode it straight into a red sunset. The resulting explosion flared into the Japanese battle flag which sank slowly below the horizon, indicating Goofy had sunk the entire Japanese fleet. The picture was released during the war and got a lot of laughs, but had to be shelved after peace was declared.

One day, when Walt came into my room, I began to explain my story, but I soon saw he wasn't interested. Suddenly, he said, "I want you to get on the South American stuff and help them out."

I said , "I don't want to, Walt. I'm happy here on the shorts."

"I don't care if you're happy on the shorts," he snapped, "I want you to work on the South American stuff and give them a lift."

I was on the point of saying I didn't want to make the trip, but wisely thought better of it.

My reception from the newly-returned group was frigid, and I could understand. They had just completed a great three-month vacation-like tour of South America and were having a tough time settling down to work. But Walt, impatient as usual, expected a rush of fresh ideas, and, upset by the lack of progress, had tossed me into the pot to stir the stew. After making the rounds and assuring everybody I didn't want to work with them, but was forced to, I returned to my room to find the walls barren. *My How to Be a Sailor* story had already been sent downstairs to the Director's Unit.

After sitting for awhile in the empty room, thinking and not coming up with anything, I made the rounds of the South American unit again, hoping to find something that would inspire me. It was not until I dropped into Zaire's room that something clicked. She had pinned a few watercolor sketches of scenes, characters, and animals to her storyboards, and they would inspire anybody, for she was a very fine artist. I was intrigued with a watercolor sketch she had made of a rope suspension bridge stretching across a Bolivian mountain gorge, and another sketch of a little Bolivian boy playing a flute, pinned next to a drawing of a big llama. The three sketches inspired me to create a cartoon of Donald Duck as an American tourist in the Lake Titicaca region. He blundered around with his camera and finally rented a llama for a trip into the mountain country. He rode the llama horseback style, and halfway across a rope suspension bridge high above a deep gorge, the llama balked. Donald got off his back and in a temper kicked him in the fanny, but the llama wouldn't budge. Donald, in a rage, attempted to make the big animal move. Suddenly, he began to walk but loosened the slats, and Donald frantically tried to replace them, shouting for the uncooperative beast to stop. Donald finally tumbled into the lake and was last seen drifting away, his fanny stuck in a big native jug.

Walt and the group had visited the Argentine pampas and shot 16-millimeter scenes of cowboys (gauchos). Goofy was used as an American cowboy attempting to accustom himself to the life of a gaucho. A narrator described the gaucho's clothes, and, as each item was mentioned, it appeared on Goofy, ending with him holding a boleadoras, the Argentine lasso. The bolas (for short) consisted of several heavy silver balls attached to the ends of leather thongs. The gaucho whirled this contraption above his head like a lasso and would throw it with great accuracy. The whirling bolas could trip up a running steer or an ostrich. Goofy got himself and his horse hopelessly tangled up when he tried to use it.

Walt had brought a famous Argentine artist[19] up to the studio to make sure our Pampas scenes and gaucho costumes would be authentic.

The artist was a compact little man, bursting with energy and enthusiasm. He drew and painted in a frenzy, scattering his work over the desk and floor. Behind his back, fellows ridiculed his work because it was not cute in the Disney style. But he was a primitive, and his drawing, though seeming crude, was not to be imitated.

Early in April 1942, he gave a lecture in Projection Room 3, C-11 on "Gauchos and Customs of the Argentine". Among other things, he gave a demonstration of how to swing a bolas, which he had with him. He became wildly excited whirling them above his head, narrowly missing the ceiling sprinkler system, while we ducked under our seats trying to think what "stop" was in Spanish.

Saludos Amigos was released in February 1943, during the World War, and was very successful, creating much-needed good will between South America and the United States.

When the picture was previewed, I was surprised to see my name appear on the screen in large letters heading up the story credits, while the names of those making the trip with Walt were billed in smaller letters as "Story Researchers". I think he had my name appear first and in large type not to reward me but to send a message to the "Group" showing his displeasure with them for not producing stories faster, after returning from their long, free trip. This was Walt's way, and, as I've said before, he was not the man to spare anyone's feelings. His apparent generosity did me more harm than good among my fellow employees.

Walt was really impressed with people who had a college education because he didn't. He took a fancy to certain people and promoted them, though they might not know anything about the work.

One of these was Muggle, a little man built like a puffer pigeon. His face, by nature, was not intended to be of a smiling aspect, and he strutted about the studio with an etastic step, giving the appearance of importance on the move. He was invited to join the Penthouse Club, located on the top floor of the main building. Along with other members, he took his lunch there and was soon discovered to be of a deadly serious nature, a perfect subject for gags.

One afternoon I returned from lunch early and visited with Riley the cop on the main gate.[20] He was a big, friendly Irishman, well liked by everybody. Muggle drove in, and, stopping in front of Riley's window, said, "Mr Muggle is in." Riley said, "Okay, Muggle."

The little man got out of his car, and, approaching Riley in his pompous manner, said, "The name is Mr. Muggle." Riley said, "Okay, Muggle." Muggle returned to his car in a huff, and, slamming the door, sped into the parking lot and got a ticket from Riley for speeding on the lot.

When Walt had gone to New York to take bows on *Fantasia*, the fellows saw an opportunity to have some fun at Muggle's expense and suggested that he was the one best able to phrase a telegram congratulating Walt on the success of *Fantasia*, although the critics had not exactly raved over the picture.

Before sending the telegram, Muggle wanted all members of the Penthouse Club to add their names to it. But after reading the telegram with straight faces, they decided it would be better to sign it as a group.

I wouldn't have cared to be within hearing distance of Walt when he read this:

> "Dear Walt: Your old gang back here is tickled pink by the grand reception given *Fantasia* and we want you to know that each and every one of us who are closest to you join with the critics and the public in acclaiming *Fantasia* as your personal triumph. Without your patient and guiding hand in every detail of the production we would never have been able to play our parts. We are not letting the applause and the glory go to our heads, for we know you will come back with bigger and better plans that will demand still harder work. Bravo, Walt—lead on, and we will follow you to new victories."
>
> THE PENTHOUSE BOYS

Chapter Eleven

During 1942, the studio was taken over by the government in order to make training films for the armed forces.

One of these films was *Rules of the Nautical Road*, written by a lieutenant commander[21]. Since an animated film was to be based on his book, Walt brought the commander down from Seattle to oversee production.

This was a hectic time of shipbuilding and war materiel manufacturing. Hotel rooms in Los Angeles were practically impossible to get, and, as the commander was without a car, Walt kindly offered him the use of his private office sleeping quarters, which also had cooking facilities. The commander, unfortunately, turned out to be a frugal man, and instead of eating his meals in the studio restaurant as expected, he cooked them in Walt's office, which threw Walt into a foul mood. His office, where he received high-ranking officials, stank of fried onions, a favorite dish of the commander's.

After the success of *Saludos Amigos*, Walt wanted to make a picture on Mexico, combining, for the first time, live-action footage with animated cartoon stories, and it would be a goodwill gesture to our touchy Mexican friends, who felt they should have been included in *Saludos Amigos*.

Dill, by now a story-sketch man, and I were ordered to begin researching material for the picture, but we soon discovered the library and historic Olivera Street in Los Angeles yielded few ideas, and we began to run travel pictures of Mexico every evening in Projection Room 3-C-12, adjacent to Walt's office.

The commander dropped in, in his stocking feet, to view the pictures with us. He usually took a seat near Walt, and, lighting his pipe in a leisurely manner, blew out clouds of choking smoke, which drove Walt up the wall. He hated pipe smokers, he said, because they wasted too much time, knocking out the ashes, refilling their pipes, tamping down the tobacco, lighting and relighting "the damn things".

After a half dozen smoky evenings of this, Walt called a halt to the travelogues and decided a visit to Mexico would be more productive, and so a Mexican unit was formed.

Three of us were ordered to be an advance unit, and, after receiving typhoid shots, etc., etc., we departed for Mexico City on the evening of December 4, 1942, aboard an old DC-3 Pan American Airways plane. (No large commercial planes were in operation at that time.) We went ahead to make sure Walt got the Presidential Suite at the Reforma Hotel, the best in Mexico City. A larger group would arrive later.[22]

We landed the next afternoon, after a tiring, thirteen-hour flight. The air had become very thin as the plane climbed to 14,000 feet in order to clear the mountains ringing the city. Breathing was difficult, and the pilot's jolly voice came over the intercom suggesting we passengers hold our breaths for a couple of minutes and he would be "over the hill". But none of us had any breath left to hold, and the stewardess, in the nick of time, passed out little ampoules which you broke open by pressing thumb and forefinger together, and inhaling the contents which gave immediate relief.

The head of the Mexican Tourist Bureau met us at the airport and escorted us to the Reforma, where our business manager reserved the Presidential Suite and some twelve rooms.

The incoming staff would occupy rooms on several floors. Mine was number 419. The office was on the 7th floor, next to Walt's suite, and a pretty senorita, who spoke a flock of languages fluently, was engaged as secretary.

Walt, his wife, and the remaining party arrived later, and we went out to the airport in a driving rain storm to meet them.

As the incoming plane circled the city, Walt made a speech, but static caused by lightning scrambled it up so bad, you couldn't make heads nor tails of it.

A soggy Mariachi band, playing their instruments upside down to keep from melting the strings, greeted the deplaning passengers with music that gurgled as if being played under water.

Walt got off the plane looking like one of the thunder clouds, and, paying no attention to all the fuss and ado, demanded to be driven to the hotel.

He didn't seem to be in good spirits all during his stay in Mexico, and

I think he might have had the "turistas" [traveler's diarrhea] off and on.

The storm passed over, and across a vast green plain stood Mexico's two famous snowcapped mountains, Popocatepetl and his sleeping lady friend, Iztaccihuatl. Nowhere in the world will you see a sight surpassing it.

For the next few days we toured the city, including the Palace of Fine Arts. After climbing a long flight of marble stairs, I almost fell back down them out of surprise, for facing me was a larger-than-life size painting of a beautiful girl imparting to a ragged, old, bewhiskered beggar the milk he was badly in need of, in the same way an infant gets his nourishment.

The floating gardens of Xochimilco were a must. They were situated a short distance from Mexico City at the head of the old Viga Canal, renowned from Cortez' time.

On a Sunday, we drove out to the Gardens, accompanied by motorcycle cops. En route, a chauffeur-driven limousine without license plates passed us at high speed. I called to one of the cops, "Why don't you arrest that crazy guy?" He pulled over, and, shrugging his shoulders, shouted, "ES EL GENERAL!", indicating the General could drive as he pleased.

Just as we parked at Xochimilco, a streetcar packed with riders skidded to a stop nearby. It seemed impossible to jam so many people into one little streetcar, and I watched them stream out. The one man operator ran to a little refreshment stand, and, buying a quart bottle of beer, drained it in one long gulp, dashed back to his car, burping loudly, shifted the trolley, grabbed the controls, ran to the other end, and, fitting them into place, sped away, bells clanging like mad.

Our guide directed us to a pavilion overlooking the floating gardens. We refreshed ourselves while taking pictures of the canals and the clusters of flat-bottomed roofed-over boats bearing names such as "Lolita", "Conchita", "Alicia", etc., etc. There seemed to me to be too many commercial banners over the foot bridges advertising beer and Hennessy brandy.

The boats, full of picnickers, were poled leisurely along the canals, while their occupants enjoyed tacos and beer, leaving a trail of empty bottles and paper bags bobbing along behind them.

Marimba bands, mariachi bands, and guitar singers floated along behind the boats playing separate tunes with gusto at the same time. As they glided alongside picnickers, they held out sombreros for gratuities.

Mexico City's flowers and vegetables came from Xochimilco. A glance at the murky waters made you stop and think before enjoying a beautiful salad. Unfortunately, some of us didn't.

The next morning, a couple of us were in the midst of breakfast in the hotel coffee shop, when Walt came along and said he was going out to the rifle range to watch the police practice fancy shooting. He asked if we wanted to go along.

We got up and went, leaving our breakfasts unfinished, becaus you didn't exactly suggest to Walt to sit down and wait while you dealt with food.

We had been fortunate to arrive in Mexico at the time of the Festival of Guadalupe. The big, pink cathedral was the most sacred shrine of the Mexican people, rich and poor alike. Crowds of people milled around in front of the cathedral to watch the dancers, all barefoot, who had traveled hundreds of miles from outlying states, to reach the shrine on this sacred day and perhaps be fortunate to get a glimpse of the precious impression of the Virgin of Guadalupe, said to have been made on the apron of Don Diego when he was instructed by the Virgin to build this cathedral.

Our group, headed by Walt, reached an area where we had a good view of the dancers, all wretchedly poor, carrying heavy banners and clad in colorful costumes representing their states. The dance was performed in a big circle, in single file, each dancer doing his thing, which seemed to be a sort of 1-2-3-hop, 1-2-3-hop, but none of them were in step. Every now and then, a dancer flopped, exhausted by the long hike from their provinces to the cathedral. Little nurses darted up and lugged them away to the Red Cross tents.

While the monotonous dance was in full swing, a gaunt Mexican came over to us. He was clad in a black suit and wore a Stetson. His none-too-clean shirt was buttoned at the throat with a gold collar button, but lacked a tie. Displaying a lot of dental work, he grasped Walt's hand, and, shaking it vigorously, cried, "Ah, Senor Deesnay, I see you are having a good time, no!" And pointing to himself, said, "I am the senator from Hichoacan!" And, clamping his hand to his heart, exclaimed theatrically, "Ah, these dancers, they are my people, my life, my soul! Every movement speaks to me of my country, Nichoacan!" Then, wringing Walt's hand warmly, he cried, "Adios!", and melted into the crowd before Walt could get a word in.

The dancing continued, and soon another Mexican wearing the same black suit, the same Stetson, and in need of a shave, came over, and introducing himself, cried, "I see you are Senor Deesnay and me, I am the senator from Oaxaca." And, pointing to the very same dancers his colleague had claimed were from Nichoacan, exclaimed, "These are my people all from Oaxaca! In Mexico are many states, but these", stabbing a finger at the hopping bunch coming around again, he cried, "they speak of the very soul of my native state!"

Walt frowned, "Another senator just now said they are from Nichoacan!"

The second senator reacted as if he had been stabbed through the heart.

"No-no-no!" he cried. "Who tell you that, Senor Deesnay, is wrong!"

And with an "Adios!", faded into the crowd.

Seeing the first senator a few minutes later, Walt called to him. He came beaming. "Another senator just told me these dancers are from Oaxaca, not Michoacan, as you said," exclaimed Walt.

The first senator shrugged, as if to say, "Maybe so," and, after pumping Walt's hand vigorously and telling him to have a good time, melted into the milling crowd.

"What the hell," Walt snapped, angrily. "Why don't these birds get their act together!"

We agreed, but from Walt's expression saw he was in no mood for any remarks from us.

Dill nudged me, and there was Muddle standing close to Walt, making his usual little sketches and showing them to him. Walt nodded and looked around at us, annoyed, as if to say, "What the hell's the matter with you guys?"

That evening, several of us had dinner at Sanborns where Dill called Muddle a "kiss-ass", and Muddle, who was of a ruddy complexion, and looking like a candidate for a stroke, leaned angrily toward Dill, who remained calm and smiling, and announced in restrained anger he was about to beat the crap out of him. Dill, still all smiles, said in a low voice, "I wouldn't do that if I were you, Muddle." And something in the intonation of Dill's voice jogged Muddle's memory, and it must have come to mind that Dill had once been a boxer. That was the only way I could account for Muddle's sudden departure, leaving us to pick up his dinner check. But, that was no problem, as we had been given a liberal supply of funds.

This unusual generosity gave me an uneasy feeling, for Walt, in my experience, had not been known to have any connection with that word, and I expected a mistake had been made. I was reassured later when I learned that our trip was financed by good old Uncle Sam.

The Tourist Bureau took us to see the annual Christmas dance at the exclusive Spanish Club. We entered to find floors of red marble and large vases covered with gold filigree work and filled with scented roses, all tastefully arranged around the large room. Strains of dance music came from the floor above, and we followed Walt up the richly carpeted, brass-bound stairs to the second floor, a huge lavishly decorated area, where two dance orchestras played Strauss waltzes. Beautifully gowned senoritas whirled around the floor in the arms of their escorts, while, seated in comfortable chairs lining the walls, plump, gimlet-eyed, stern-visaged duanas, wearing lace mantillas, watched the young ladies with hawk-like intensity to make sure sufficient air space separated them from their partners.

During the dance, a charming Spanish lady came up to Walt, and, holding out a card, said, "Senor Deesnay, you please to draw for me thee Meeckee Mouse?"

"I leave that to my staff," he replied, and looked around, probably for Muddle, but for once he wasn't there, and the rest of us had moved back into the crowd, forcing Walt to make the drawing himself. I went up and looked over his shoulder while he scrawled his big signature across the bottom half of the card. I saw that he had made a God-awful drawing of an old *Steamboat Willie*-type Mickey, with the pipestem legs and a long tail. He returned the card to the lady. She looked at it in astonishment and then back at Walt with a confused expression, and said, "Thees ees Meeckee Mouse?"

"What do you think?" he said, curtly.

I cleared out then and there, and taxied back to the hotel. It would have been dangerous to cross Walt's path that night.

We went to a round of cocktail parties and dinners and were interviewed by the press.

Of all our parties, Mr. Harry Wright's invitation to dinner and a viewing of his large collection of 16-millimeter pictures of Mexico was the best. Mr. Wright, an American, had first come to Mexico in 1904 and had become a millionaire.[23]

Walt didn't show up that evening and we, "El Grupo," as the Mexicans referred to us, went in his place. Hearing that Mr. Wright was a teetotaler, we dropped by the University Club to fortify ourselves against a boring evening.

His mansion, an imposing and weathered stone structure, was surrounded by a high, spiked, iron fence and seemed remote and deserted. But, after ringing the gate bell a half dozen times, a white-clad Mexican servant appeared and let us in.

Mr. Wright, a stout, dignified man of some sixty years, met us at the front door, shook hands all around, and asked us to follow him down a long corridor. The walls were covered with pictures and plaques. He guided us into an enormous room where a large map of the world was mounted on a tripod just inside the door.

Mr. Wright pressed a button and the map lit up, and, in large letters spreading over it, spelled HARRY WRIGHT'S WORLD TOURS. The letters faded out and a thin orange ribbon of light appeared, slithering like a snake across the map, tracing Mr. Wright's various trips. Then the ribbon of light vanished and the routine was repeated, like one of those neon signs lighting up a hamburger drive-in.

The room was enormous and held an amazing collection. One item alone was a brand-new unpainted Japanese sampan (fishing boat) at least forty feet long and mounted on chocks to keep it from capsizing. It was apparent Mr. Wright didn't collect things in a small way. Close to the sampan stood an ivory ball half the size of a man carved all over with lace-like designs, and, amazingly, inside it were two more balls covered with similar designs. A sign on a stand told the viewer that Mr. Wright had acquired it while traveling in India, and the ball was said to be over six hundred years old. The carvings must have taken a couple of centuries to complete. How the feat was accomplished remains one of antiquity's mysteries.

Along the walls of the theater were hung priceless Persian rugs. Jade Buddahs of various colors and sizes ranged along the wall beneath them, and attached to each Buddah was a card giving the dynasty from which it came and where Mr. Wright had purchased it.

Finally, he consulted his watch and said we had just enough time before dinner to sign the guest book. We did, adding sketches of Disney characters and trite comments such as "You can't go wrong with Wright."

Mrs. Wright, a gray-haired lady with a solemn face illumined by a pair of keen gray eyes, joined us, and we sat down to a gourmet dinner served on ex-President Diaz' solid gold dinner service, which Mr. Wright said he had acquired in 1911 after his friend, the ex-president, had been forced to flee Mexico.

All during the meal, Mr. Wright took over the conversation, giving us an endless, boring account of his numerous golf games with Ambassador Josephus Daniels. Mr. Wright's wife corrected him whenever he got off the track, which was every few minutes.

But, in spite of his wanderings, the food made up for the tedious stretches of autobiography.

Although the old mansion was no different on the outside from its neighbors, it was filled with many surprises. His Krall Theater was an eye-boggler and could accommodate one hundred and fifty guests in red velvet upholstered reclining seats made especially for him in Egypt.

Along one wall was painted a mural of an African countryside with a lake and mountains in the distance. In the foreground, a couple of lions made short work of a zebra.

Along the opposite walls were painted life-sized African natives—a platter-lipped Ubangi girl, a Matabel beauty with a screwy hairdo, a ricksha boy from Durban, South Africa, etc., etc.

On both sides of the movie screen were bas-reliefs of elephants, hippos, and giraffes, and lots of monkeys were sprinkled around in the trees.

Above the mural was a colorful border of the flags of 61 countries visited by the Wrights during five trips around the world. In back of the last row of seats, above an Egyptian mural stretching into the distance, camels plodded across acres of sand toward distant pyramids. On the wall a blank space had been left in case the Wrights wanted to add more flags. Mr. Wright's theater was becoming crowded with hundreds of knickknacks, like elephants' and rhinos' feet hollowed out to make trash baskets.

Sitting on a platform beneath the movie screen was a large alabaster reproduction of the Taj Mahal. Soon, Mr. Wright's collection would make it difficult to climb into a seat in the Krall Theater.

A part of his vast collection of 16-millimeter films of Mexico was shown to us. And we saw Xochimilco over again, this time in the summer when flowers bloomed all over the lake in a profusion of beautiful colors, quite different from the drab Xochimilco we had just seen on our winter visit.

As the film unrolled, we saw ancient historical ceremonies and festive carnivals in various little towns of the emotional Mexicans.

We saw Tehuantepec, where the Tehuanas are considered some of the world's most beautiful women. The films rolled on endlessly, showing the Zacatecas who looked more like Arabs than Mexicans; the Kickapoo Indians, who wear Chinese pigtails; the Huichols, who get high on a drug made from the cactus, called peyote; the Diaper-Men of Chiapas; Tarascan Indians hauling in their beautiful butterfly nets or killing wild ducks from dugout canoes by using long spears hurled with pre-Columbian throwing sticks; and Otomi Indians, who kill fish by biting their heads off.

On Sunday, we went to the only event in Mexico that starts on time—the bullfights. Four o'clock sharp!

Walt was seated in the choice first row seats surrounded by Mexican officials anxious to explain the techniques of their beloved bullfighting to him, and squeezed in next to Walt was Muddle, industriously sketching.

We (El Grupo) sat in cheaper seats up the aisle some six rows behind Walt. Mrs. Disney sat alone across the aisle from us. Soon after the start of the bullfights, when the picadores and the banderilleros had worked the bull into a furious rage, Walt began looking around restlessly and finally spotted his wife. He beckoned angrily for her to join him, and, turning to Muddle, made a gesture I interpreted as "Get the hell out of here!" He quickly vacated his seat, and, coming up the aisle, ignored our grins and took a seat nearby.

The arena was packed with spectators who rocked it with thunderous cries of "Ole! Ole!" whenever a matador made a particularly spectacular piece of cape work and avoided losing his life by inches.

Five brave bulls died that afternoon, and the sixth was put out of his misery by the star of the show, a swarthy, dark little man clad in a gold-embroidered pink velvet suit. He strutted arrogantly out onto the yellow sand and proceeded to give a flawless performance, being nearly killed several times, which won the hearts of his countrymen. He finally dispatched the bull by going in over the horns, the most dangerous way, and the crowd went crazy rocking the stands with applause. The matador was given the highest award, both ears and the tail.

He made several rounds of the arena waving the bloody objects over his head, and at this the crowd, already in a frenzy, went absolutely crazy and threw coats, hats, gloves, shawls into the ring, and I think only the cold afternoon kept them from throwing in all of their clothes. The articles were tossed back into the stands by the matador and his assistants. And so concluded a regular Sunday performance at the bullfights.

Our trip came to an end. We flew back to Burbank bursting with ideas for our Mexican picture.

We came up with a fast-shooting Mexican charro (cowboy) rooster and named him Panchito. He took his new friends, José Carioca, the Brazilian parrot, and Donald Duck on a tour of Mexico on his flying serape.

The Three Caballeros, when released, was well-received by the public.

As usual throughout production, Walt never flagged in his striving for perfection, cutting out footage, adding footage, even watching and changing color gradation, as additional cels were added to a scene so that color values throughout remained constant.

It took a strong, dominant character to do this, and Walt was it! And, as usual, without regard to costs.

Then he began complaining that costs were running up, saying he walked around his swimming pool half the night, his head ringing like a cash register: "$920,000-$930,000-$940,000."

After Walt left the meeting, Dodger the producer said he could have finished the picture a lot sooner and cheaper if Walt had stayed out of it. It was one of those things somebody says in anger

One of Walt's lackeys reported the comment to Walt, and he cornered Dodger in the hall with the story. Dodger faced up to it and admitted he had said it. Walt never forgave him.

One morning, Walt called me up and said Mr. Wright was in town from New York on his way home to Mexico and was very anxious to see *The Three Caballeros*. He would be in at two o'clock, and I was to set up a screening for him in Projection Room 3 C-12.

At two o'clock, I met Mr. Wright in Walt's office and took him to the Projection Room. We sat together for awhile discussing his Krall Theater and the help his 16-millimeter pictures had given us. After a few minutes, the projectionist called down from his booth, "All set", and I said, "Okay, roll it", and the lights went out. Lively Mexican music accompanied the title and credits. The picture had been running for several minutes when Walt slipped into a seat next to Mr. Wright and asked him how he liked the picture. Mr. Wright's reply was a contented snore, for he had fallen asleep. In the dim yellow light cast by the projector's beam, I saw a furious expression on Walt's face. He jumped up and left the room. Nobody, but nobody, went to sleep during his pictures!

The picture ran on for seventy minutes, and, when it ended, Mr. Wright continued to snore peacefully. The lights came on. I nudged him gently and he came awake. After mumbling a bit, he turned to me and said, "Wonderful, delightful. I don't think I've ever enjoyed anything more."

I never knew whether he meant the picture or his nap.

Several years later, Dodger's remark about *The Three Caballeros* must have still rankled Walt, for he suddenly told him to make a short subject cartoon—think up a story, draw it up, animate it, direct it—by himself. Now, Dodger was a great animator and had animated some of the funniest scenes ever done in the studio, but he was not much of a storyman. He slaved away, knowing Walt would judge his worth to the studio, not on what he had done, but on this one short cartoon.

When Walt saw the completed picture, he turned thumbs down on it. In his mind, Dodger had slipped and was no longer of value to the studio, so he terminated him. That must have been hard for Dodger to take, because he had been with Walt for thirty years, and they had been as close as Walt ever got with anybody.

I ran into Dodger after he left the studio, and we discussed it. Before parting, he said the only thing he regretted was leaving Walt without a handshake.

Years earlier, after the new studio had been built, Dodger bought a new home in the San Fernando Valley, and I was invited over one evening to see it.

Walt and his wife dropped by and we chatted for awhile. When it had been decided to play Parcheesi, I went into the kitchen and joined Sligh and his stewardess girl friend, who were having a drink.

Mrs. Disney came in and in her meek little voice reminded us, "You know Walt can't lose."

Needless to say, Walt was the big winner that night and went home in good spirits.

Another incident illustrating Walt's refusal to be second best was related to me by Loganbary, a special effects animator and director.

He had accompanied Walt to Pebble Beach for a conference, and after dinner Walt suggested they play a game of pool. Loganbary said he beat Walt easily, and Walt, who had a short temper, bounced his pool cue off the floor, saying "Signs of a misspent youth!", and stormed from the room.

Loganbary didn't sleep a wink that night, and first thing next morning begged Walt to play another game, complimenting him on "some darn good shots" he had made, and saying he, Loganbary, had just been lucky. So they played again, and Walt won handily. The trip went off fine.

After lunch one day, I was on the third floor getting a pack of cigarettes out of the machine when Walt came pounding by, Mrs. Disney a couple of paces astern of him. Walt passed without speaking, but she stopped and said, suddenly, "We have to be funny, don't we, Homer."

I was about to agree with her when Walt, who was turning into his corridor, called back, "Come on, Lilly." She said, "Yes, Walt," and hurried after him.

Lilly seldom said anything. Usually she just smiled, but when she did say anything, she was in wholehearted agreement with her husband, which is a good trait in a wife.

Chapter Twelve

Four postwar films, *Make Mine Music, Fun and Fancy Free, Melody Time*, and *Ichabod and Mr. Toad*, were hastily made to keep the studio afloat.

All his life Walt had been a perfectionist, never satisfied, always adding, changing, and discarding expensive animation footage. Now came the time when some of it could be put to use. We went to the film morgue and built those films from bits and pieces of discarded animation, adding new cartoons and combining them with live-action sequences in order to make feature films, running one hour and fifteen minutes; a demanding task.

While these pictures were in the works, my annual two weeks' vacation came due and I was enjoying myself in Seattle with a Tom Collins, when news came over the radio that Walt Disney had laid off 450 people. I almost bit my glass in two. Recovering from the shock, I telephoned the studio.

The Story Department business manager told me not to worry, I was okay. But my vacation was ruined anyway. Friends would say, "I hear they're closing down Disney's." I managed to force a grin and reply that it didn't affect me, but I could hear them saying to themselves, "Oh, yeah."

I cut my vacation short and returned to the studio. The sight of the parking lot turned my stomach, for it was almost empty. And the lights in the usually brightly lit main building dimmed, as if great dreams had diminished to 25-watt bulbs.

On my way up to my unit, I dropped into a couple of story rooms. Lights had been turned off, drawers stood half open, pens and pencils littered the desks as though the occupants had dropped everything and fled. Instantly, I was reminded of the old sailing ship, *Marie Celeste*, found in the Atlantic with all sails set, but not a living soul on board.

My room was dark and silent, and I was on the point of calling Wetmore to see if I should resume work, but before the phone had time to ring, Walt came in and sank into a chair. He seemed depressed. This was a snarled up time for him; he had gone from poverty to riches and back to poverty again. Now he was faced with a long uphill climb, and it would be harder this time because he had loaded himself with debts and a huge new studio. He stared at the storyboards, seeming to be deep in thought. He got to his feet suddenly, and, starting to leave the room, turned and said, "I can go over to MGM tomorrow and make $350,000 a year." What could I say to that? Nothing. Period.

Walt's remark was a shocker, and I sat for a long time after he left my room, thinking. *Snow White* had made him rich, but he had spent most of the profits on a new studio and then went on to make more cartoon features—*Pinocchio, Bambi, Fantasia*—all costing approximately 2 million apiece. Walt had gone on a spending spree, but it had been cut short by studio unrest, the long strike, and, finally, the loss of his lucrative foreign markets, due to the war, when he had worked without profit on government films. After the war, he had struggled to get back into peace-time markets, making short features; successful, but not bringing in those necessary millions. I understood why Walt was depressed.

During the time we were making the first short feature, Walt decided to include "Casey at the Bat" as one of the short cartoons, and he wanted E.L. Thayer's famous poem to be narrated by Jimmy Durante.

Several of us went over to see him in his apartment on Olympic Boulevard in Los Angeles. His old buddies and former vaudeville partners, Clayton and Jackson, were there, alert, watchful, suspicious.

Their attitude seemed to be, nobody is going to put anything over on our pal Jimmy. He bounced around, friendly, unrestrained, and enthusiastic, clad in a brown bath robe. On the breast pocket was stitched in yellow thread "Schnozzola", his nickname. He knew Thayer's poem and seemed anxious to do a musical recitation of it.

Several days later, Clayton came to the studio to look at the storyboards. He was a small, wiry man with a grim visage. I was reminded of a movie gangster, for he spoke like one. After running through the story, I said anxiously (for he had not cracked a smile throughout), "How do you like it?" And he said, "What's Jimmy get out'a dis?"

I said, "I don't know anything about that end of it. You'll have to go up to the third floor and talk to Casting." I dropped him off there, and that's the last I heard of Jimmy Durante.

From Clayton's attitude, he appeared to be able to speak for Jimmy.[24] Evidently, Clayton couldn't cut a satisfactory deal, or Jimmy had more lucrative commitments elsewhere. The musical recitation of "Casey At The Bat" was finally done by Jerry Colona, a big-mouth comic.

When *Make Mine Music* had been completed, we moved onto *Fun and Fancy Free*. Jiminy Cricket, the little character from *Pinocchio*, was used to tie two stories together.

The first one was about a circus bear named Bongo, based on a short story by Sinclair Lewis.

The second one was *Mickey and the Beanstalk*. We had done considerable work on this story before the Second World War, but it had been shelved in order to make way for government training films. Now a new version was to be made. We had the reels of animated film sent up from the vault and found that a lot of editing and new animation was necessary.

Walt decided to give it a new twist, combining live action with cartoons, which had been so successful in *The Three Caballeros*. Edgar Bergen and his dummies were called in. Bergen was to tell the story to a little girl, Luana Patton, and Charlie McCarthy was to interrupt and heckle him. Mortimer Snerd always got mixed up, and that would further confuse Bergen.

He came to the studio with several of his gag men, and they set to work cooking up a dialogue routine Walt would approve of.

One afternoon, I saw Bergen angrily shaking a candy machine, located in the hall next to the library doors, and I asked him what he was trying to do. "I'm trying to get a candy bar out of this machine," he said, testily. "I put a nickel in and nothing came out." (Thirty-cent candy bars were only a nickel then.) I told him to go into the library and the librarian would refund his money. He went in and got his nickel back.

The original voice of Willie the Giant in *Jack and the Beanstalk* was done by Billy Gilbert, and we had to bring him back for new recordings because his voice had changed over the years since his original recording, and a lot of retakes were needed.

Billy Gilbert was a famous old-time comedian who played heavies. He was a big, shaggy bear of a man with a deep rumbling voice, perfect for Willie the Giant. I became acquainted and invited him to lunch in the Commissary, and, after we were seated, Billy said this was only the second time he had been back in the Disney Studio since the old days when it was on Hyperion Avenue and he was the voice of the dwarf Sneezy in *Snow White*.

Billy was in a mood to reminisce, and this is what he told me:

"I heard they had some characters in mind for those *Snow White* dwarfs. I went over and met Walt and he liked my sneeze.

"Then they called me in over a long period of time to record sessions of sneezing. They had a big paper pasted up in front of the mike and I had to sneeze to each square on the paper, which represented a frame of film. One day, I had been sneezing about eight hours. It was terrible. Each sneeze right to the beat, but somehow I couldn't please that sonofabitch in charge. I can't remember his name now, and I'm glad I can't.

"Nothing pleased him. I'd sneezed until I was getting hysterical, on the verge of collapse. Everything was wrong. I was shaking all over, but this guy insisted I do a lot of retakes.

"Finally, I went over to the mike and said, 'HAVE YOU GOT PLENTY OF VOLUME IN THERE? ALL CHANNELS OPEN?' He called back, said he was all set, and I yelled 'Fuck you!' and took my coat and went home. They called me on the phone, trying to get me back, but I'd had enough. They rang up again and again, but I told them they had enough assorted sneezes to do ten pictures and I never went back."

When all work on *Make Mine Music* was finished, Mert Kibble, the production supervisor, put the film together and showed it to Walt and to all of us, in the big projection room. The first title credit read "Production Supervisor Mert Kibble", with the title zooming in tight on "Mert Kibble".

Walt sat next to him in the darkness, and when the title came on the screen, he said in a loud voice, "Mert Kibble? Who's Mert Kibble?"

In the finished print of the film was a credit that read, "Production Supervisor Mert Kibble" in tiny letters, and if you blinked you missed it.

The little features were released one by one and public acceptance was very good, but the heavy thinkers had faint praise.

These short features never were released again as complete pictures. Television had arrived and Walt had them cut up and released as shorts on his Sunday night program, *Wonderful World of Color*. So those little features brought him unexpected revenues. In the end, Walt was always lucky. The fellows said he could "fall into it and come up smelling like a rose".

Chapter Thirteen

On a Saturday morning early in 1946, I received an unexpected telephone call from the head of the Shorts Department at MGM. He asked if I would be interested in working on stories for him and offered to more than double my salary and give me a one-year contract, which would be renewable if things worked out. I agreed to meet him the following Saturday morning and discuss it with him.

I spent the weekend weighing his offer. If things worked out, it would be swell. If they didn't, I would be outside and I knew how cold it was out there, and, remembering it was said Walt never forgave anyone who left him, I decided to stay where I was and hope for better times.

But I hadn't had a raise for years and felt the time had come. On Monday morning, I went in to see Wetmore, manager of the Story Department, deciding to use MGM's offer as a lever, if necessary, but before I could bring it up, Wetmore said, "If you think you can do better some place else, we won't stand in your way."

I had been told to get out! I couldn't believe it! I wanted to hear Walt tell me that and I went up to his office, my heart thudding like a trip hammer.

Fortunately, it was early, and Walt was free. His secretary told me to go right in. Walt was hunched over the long coffee table he used for a desk, munching a doughnut.

I said, "I'm going over to MGM and I came up to say goodbye."

He looked up in surprise. "What! You've got a contract." "I know it, and it has a little time to run," I said, "but Wetmore was speaking for you when he said if I thought I could do better some place else, he wouldn't stand in my way."

"Nobody speaks for me," Walt thundered, and bellowed to his secretary, "Get Wetmore up here!" And, turning back to me, shouted, "I do my own hiring and firing!" Then Wetmore came in, out of breath.

"Did you tell Homer to go out and look for another job?" said Walt.

Cringing as if he was about to be struck, Wetmore shook his head, "No-no," he said, "I never told Homer to go elsewhere."

"You're a goddamned liar," I said.

"I'll have no profanity in my office!" cried Walt.

Then he raged at Wetmore using plenty of bad language himself. By the time he was through, Wetmore had dropped to one knee as if he was about to be knighted, still insisting he never told me to leave.

When Walt finished, he stumbled out of the office looking like he'd been left too long in a Turkish bath.

Walt turned on me, "If you try to leave," he cried, "I'll blackball you in every studio in town. You'll never get another job!"

"I was told to go," I said.

"And I'm ordering you to stay!"

I went down to my room after the scene with Walt, thinking he usually sided with management in the long run and would probably take Wetmore's word over mine. From now on I might expect the "big eye" from Walt and I thought of going over to MGM anyway, but remembered Walt never forgave anyone who left him, and that settled it. I would stay with him.

On a sunny winter day in the fall, a big meeting was held on *Peter Pan*, the next important feature Walt had scheduled for production. He presided over the meeting, and a large audience of story, animation, and technical personnel crowded the room. Many months and a great deal of money had been spent on story preparation, resulting in approximately 40 storyboards covered with beautiful pastel sketches. It was clear this story crew had left nothing to chance.

I was a story director at the time, and when the *Peter Pan* gang had finished telling it, Walt ordered me to take over the story and shape it up for the animation director and final production. In spite of the general enthusiasm, I wasn't sold on *Peter Pan*.

Ever since *Snow White* I had been thinking off and on about *Cinderella*, and now I saw a chance to avoid *Peter Pan* and exclaimed, "Walt, can't I do *Cinderella*, instead of *Peter Pan*?"

Instantly, a chorus of voices drowned me out, "It's too much like *Snow White*...It'll be a carbon copy of it! No work's been done on it, etc., etc."

The loudest objections came from the *Peter Pan* story crew. Walt glowered at me, but I carried on excitedly.

"I want to do something with heart. There's no heart in *Peter Pan*. The way I see *Cinderella*, the audience will be involved, they'll sympathize with her, and take her side against the mean stepmother and her cat, who never gives up trying to catch Cinderella's only friends, the mice. Then the two ugly stepsisters do their best to make her life miserable." I finished by saying, "I don't see *Cinderella* as being anything like *Snow White*."

I looked around at a circle of stony faces. Walt slouched in his chair, staring absently at the *Peter Pan* storyboards. He sat up suddenly, and, to the surprise of everybody, said, "All right, go ahead with *Cinderella*. It won't take any more time to work it out than this thing." (Meaning *Peter Pan*.)

He left the room abruptly and I followed him into the hall, leaving a beehive of voices buzzing behind me. Walt stopped and turned around. "Who do you want to work with?"

"Pophoff. We get along fine."

Walt nodded and turned into his corridor, and I went downstairs to tell Pophoff about his new assignment. He had been supplying stories for a shorts director, and was glad to collaborate on the feature.

After lunch, we sat in my room and stared at the empty storyboards trying to think how to proceed. A search of the morgue for material proved fruitless, except for a signed drawing of the Prince, by Kinch, one of the studio producers, and an old, rejected live-action script written by a Hollywood screenwriter and Sligh.

We got a kick out of Kinch's scrawny Prince, which he had taken the time to color. I tacked it to a storyboard.

Realizing we had to start from scratch, we began outlining the continuity and blocking out sequences. We had covered two storyboards with printed slips when Wetmore called up. If it was okay with us, he was moving Sligh in. I covered the phone and told Pophoff. He reacted violently.

"No way!" he exclaimed. "Sligh's a smoothy. I've known him a lot longer than you have and he'll end up by getting us." I called Wetmore and said we didn't want him.

"There's nothing for him right now," said Wetmore. "If you don't want him, we'll have to lay him off."

"Lay Sligh off? After all these years and the job he's had?"

"Not any more," said Wetmore.

Sligh had given me my chance and I felt obligated, so I agreed to take him into our unit, in spite of Pophoff's objections. He was very much against it, and reminded me of the time Walt had one of his "mad-ons" against Sligh and removed him as head of the Story Department.

We had found him in a small room on the second floor working on a short by himself. The fellows felt sorry for him and pitched in and helped him gag up his story. When he'd finished it and the picture was produced, it was okay, but was said to have cost more than any short subject made up to that time. Pophoff said we had done enough for Sligh. He had survived Walt's "mad-ons", and, up until Wetmore called, had worked his way back into Walt's good graces by drifting around among the story units offering advice.

Now he moved in with us, and we finished a rough continuity on *Cinderella* and sent it up to Walt. He asked for story treatment. We sent that up, too, and he came down and went over it with us, and then gave us the okay to move ahead and take over quarters in a big unit on the third floor. We were free to add sketch and layout help as needed.

Our new unit was a whole separate wing and consisted of some ten rooms. Pophoff and I selected a large sunny room in an alcove off the hall, which we thought would accommodate Sligh as well, but, when the desks and storyboards had been moved in, he thought it was too crowded and said he would take a small office next door, but it turned out to be located at the far end of the hall.

"He's made his first move," Pophoff warned. "See how he's placed his desk right in the open doorway facing the entrance? When Walt comes in, he can't help but see him first and he'll go straight down the hall to Sligh's office."

"Ah, let's forget about it, Pophoff. He can't hurt us."

"The hell he can't," Pophoff said, angrily.

I realized this was our big chance and vowed to make *Cinderella* the best feature yet, and our enthusiasm spilled over onto the fellows, and we made that story hum.

Studio personnel began dropping in, and one of our first visitors was Kinch. When he saw his drawing tacked to a storyboard, he ripped it off in silence, and, tearing it up, tossed it into the waste basket and left the room.

Pophoff said, "I've just made a friend."

Chapter Fourteen

Barely four months after Walt told me to go ahead with *Cinderella*, a big meeting was held on it in the big projection room.

The room was crowded with producers, animators, assistants, story, layout, and background personnel.

Walt presided, and Crock, a clerk at the time, took an extensive Gallup-type poll to get the audience reaction.

A similar meeting had been held the day before on *Alice in Wonderland*. Evidently, Walt was trying to make up his mind between the two stories.

Cinderella won, hands down, and after Crock had tabulated the results of the poll, he had a report of 26 pages. Excerpts of the report follow:

> "In answer to the question, please frankly describe your impressions and feelings concerning the story of *Cinderella*."

Here are a few of the comments:

> "Beautiful adaptation. Creates a wonderful reaction which has not been evident in a cartoon feature since *Snow White*."

> "Although it's an old story, I think it has been interpreted in a very new and entertaining way that is enjoyable."

> "I think it's going to be the best picture made by Disney."

> "I think it's terrific."

> "Very good. Could be another *Snow White*."

> "I think the story, as it is now, is good and should not be changed in any way."

> "I think it is very good. It is about time we got back in the old swing of good full-length animated pictures."

> "I think it will make a wonderful picture...another *Snow White*, even better."

> "Frankly, I think it's a wonderful story. The ideas for the story are terrific and I am sure it would easily equal, if not excel, the popularity

of *Snow White*, which I think is the best picture Disney every made."

"Very good!! ...held my interest throughout the storyboard talk."

"I feel that the story, as it stands, is very entertaining and has excellent suspense."

"Better than *Snow White*. About the best done."

We continued to work hard, elated by the audience reaction. On January 15, 1948, barely four months after the first meeting, we had another big one on *Cinderella*.

[Homer tells the story from the boards.]

Roy [Disney]: Sure loaded with business.

Walt: Yes...I think the thing we have gained at this stage is the fact that all the little characters we use can play a part in the story. That is that the mice can play a definite part—the dog and the horse and all—every character is a part of the story...There's a time when you can gag a thing and times when you have to carry a certain sincere feeling if you want the story to hold.

Kipper: It's a good outline of the general plot, though.

Walt: That's right; if you follow it through step by step, it has wonderful potentials.

Links: I thought the story was very good. It seemed to tell right all the way thru.

The discussion went on, mostly by Walt, for eighteen long pages of notes.

After the meeting broke up, and we were leaving the room, Roy Disney put his arm around my shoulders and said, "Homer, that's the best thing since *Snow White*."

Walt was directly behind us, and I turned to smile at him. He glared at me and walked away.

A short time after the meeting, Pophoff and I were called into Wetmore's office. He smiled, winked confidentially, and dropped the bomb. "Walt wants you two to split up, take separate rooms on the second floor, and work on short subjects."

I was stunned, unable to speak.

Pophoff flushed an angry red. "Who's taking over *Cinderella*?" he demanded.

"For the time being, Sligh's heading up the unit," said Wetmore.

Pophoff looked at me. "What did I tell you?" he said.

I looked away. I had the sickening feeling of dropping in an elevator suddenly out of control.

Walt had run true to form. He had broken up another successful story team.

It wasn't long until we left the studio.[25]

Walt would go on like a ship beating against the wind, leaving a turbulent wake behind him.

Homer Brightman in 1935

Homer Brightman: Life After Disney

by Alberto Becattini

After fifteen years, Homer Brightman left the Disney Studio in 1950. By then, the 48-year-old Brightman was more than willing to enjoy the privileges of freelance work.

Taking a breather from animation, he showed up at the Western Printing offices in Beverly Hills, and was put under special contract to write stories for Western's line of comic books. Brightman was no newcomer to the comics field. In fact, as reported by writer Bob Karp's widow Mary Jim[26], late in 1937 Brightman had written gags for the first two months' releases of the Donald Duck newspaper strip drawn by Al Taliaferro, before Bob Karp became its regular writer. Also, he was accustomed to drawing animation storyboards—a method he would continue using for his comic book stories.

One of the first stories he penned for Western was *Mickey Mouse and the Disappearing Island*, which appeared in 1950 in the first of a few "Wheaties Premiums" and which was—curiously enough—the only Disney comic drawn by another former Disney animation writer, Don R. Christensen. It was during this period that Brightman sort of re-united with his friends, all former Disney animators and storymen. As Jack Bradbury recalled, "Jim [Davis], Al Hubbard, Hubie Karp and I decided to share an office together. [Eventually we moved] into an office in downtown Glendale. Owen Fitzgerald, a layout artist, was there for a while, too. Ken Hultgren still worked at home, but he and writer Homer Brightman came around nearly every day to lunch with us."[27]

Brightman continued writing Disney stories for Western's comic book titles, off and on, until 1970. From 1962 onwards, though, he concentrated on the stories which were being produced in connection with the Disney Studio to be released overseas. Besides several Duck stories, which often featured Rockerduck, Uncle Scrooge's adversary created by Carl Barks in 1961, he wrote a number of yarns starring Zorro, the masked avenger who had acquired new popularity thanks to the 1957-59 Disney TV series starring Guy Williams. These were short yet original stories, in which the corpulent Sergeant Garcia often stole the scene from the titular hero, drawn by Richard "Sparky" Moore, Dan Spiegle, Mel Keefer, and Jesse Marsh, among others. It is more than likely that Brightman also scripted the four short *Zorro* stories that appeared in *Walt Disney's Comics and Stories* during 1963, with art by Nat Edson.

For Western, Brightman also wrote a few Disney children's books featuring Goofy, Uncle Scrooge, and Mary Poppins, which were issued under the Whitman imprint during 1963-65.

By early 1952, Brightman was back to writing for theatrical animation. At Disney, he had always been part of a team of writers which included Harry Reeves, Carl Barks, Jack Hannah, Ted Sears, Rex Cox, Jesse Marsh, and others. Now he was going to enjoy the pleasure of being on his own, giving full vent to his ability at creating gags. He went to Walter Lantz Productions, initially working for director Don Patterson, whom he had known at Disney (Patterson had been a Disney animator from 1937 to 1945). The first Lantz short he contributed to, *The Great Who-Dood-It* starring Woody Woodpecker, was released on October 20, 1952. Strictly on a freelance basis, Brightman would be Lantz's main story-man for the next seventeen years (with a few pauses in the 1960s). Besides tackling the feats of the feisty woodpecker, Brightman helped develop the series starring the elderly hillbilly couple Maw and Paw (a cartoon spin-off of Universal's successful 1947-57 film series) for director Paul J. Smith (another former Disney animator), writing three of the four shorts they were in. Again with Smith, in 1953 he developed the penguin Chilly Willy (drawing inspiration from Pablo, the Cold-Blooded Penguin he had co-created for Disney's *The Three Caballeros*). Whether they were directed by Smith, or by Tex Avery, Alex Lovy, Jack Hannah, or Sid Marcus, Brightman wrote most of the *Chilly Willy* shorts until 1969.

Other Lantz series benefited from Brightman's contributions. *Maggie and Sam* was about the comedic misadventures of a husband

and a wife. Three shorts were produced in 1956-57, and Brightman wrote all of them for director Alex Lovy.

In 1956, Brightman thought up the country bear Windy and his son Breezy, who made their debut in the 1957 Woody Woodpecker cartoon *Fodder and Son*, directed by Paul J. Smith. The same team was responsible for the other four shorts starring the bears, which were released in 1958-59.

Upon his arrival at Lantz in 1959, former Disney director Jack Hannah was asked to come up with new characters. One he created was the diminutive, moustachioed Inspector Willoughby. The two Willoughby shorts that Brightman wrote, *Rough & Tumbleweed* and *Mississippi Slow Boat*, were not directed by Hannah, though, but by Paul J. Smith.

Still in 1959, Brightman conjured up no less than three characters for the same theatrical short. In *Space Mouse*, directed by Alex Lovy and released on September 7 that year, a highly-sophisticated cat named Doc was introduced along with two mice named Hickory and Dickory that Doc tried to capture and sell to NASA for laboratory tests. The trio appeared together in another two shorts, *Mouse Trapped* (1959) and *Witty Kitty* (1960), likewise directed by Lovy and written by Brightman. In 1956, Lovy also directed the one *Homer Pigeon* cartoon written by Brightman, *Pigeon Holed*.

By October 1957, Walter Lantz's cartoons were also seen on television in *The Woody Woodpecker Show*, which aired on ABC for a year. The program, hosted by Walter Lantz himself, just reran theatrical shorts, but there were special feature segments in which Brightman appeared alongside writer Dalton Sandifer, directors Alex Lovy and Paul J. Smith, animator Laverne Harding, and background artist Raymond Jacobs.

As an aside, Brightman also wrote the dialogue and stories for *Woody Woodpecker's Family Album*, a 33 1/3 rpm record released by Decca in 1957. Besides Woody Woodpecker, it also featured Andy Panda, Oswald the Rabbit, Homer Pigeon, Chilly Willy, Sad Cuckoo, and Pepito.

Although the one hundred and four theatrical shorts Brightman scripted for Lantz made up the bulk of his workload from 1952-69, he was so prolific that other Hollywood cartoon studios benefited from his talents through those years. As of 1956, he started contributing to MGM shorts. When Bill Hanna and Joe Barbera decided to give the bulldog Spike and his little son Tyke their own cartoon series, Brightman was entrusted with the scripts, although only two shorts were produced. Mike Lah directed the four shorts that Brightman wrote with the diminutive, long-faced dog Droopy during 1958. The last cartoon Brightman penned for MGM, *Tot Watchers*, was also the first *Tom and Jerry* short for which a writer was ever credited—and the last to be released after MGM had shut down its animation department in the spring of 1957.

During the late 1950s and 1960s, Brightman also tackled TV animation with relative ease. In 1957-58, he scripted fifty two episodes of the *Bozo the Clown* TV series. Larry Harmon had purchased the licensing rights to the character from Capitol Records in 1956, and three years later a cartoon series was released which would remain in syndication for decades. Time and again, Brightman would recycle gags–and more. One *Bozo* episode entitled *Papoose on the Loose* shared its title and themes with a 1961 Walter Lantz "Cartune".

Another film producer, Henry G. Saperstein, purchased UPA from Steve Bosustow in 1959, entering the field of TV cartoons but soon losing its reputation for quality. Among the series UPA produced, there was one based on Chester Gould's famous newspaper-strip detective, Dick Tracy, titled *The Adventures of Dick Tracy* or *The Dick Tracy Show*. First syndicated in 1961, it was a far cry from its hard-boiled comic counterpart. Brightman penned twenty-six five-minute episodes, helping create such original if dim-witted members of Tracy's team as Jo Jitsu, Hemlock Holmes, and Heap O'Calory.

On December 20, 1965, *The New Three Stooges* made its debut in syndication, produced by Norman Maurer's company Normandy III with Cambria Animation Studios, which had been founded by former comic artist Clark Haas with Edwin Gillette and Dick Brown in 1957. Starring Moe Howard, Larry Fine, and Joe "Curly" DeRita, *The New Three Stooges* combined live-action and animated segments to tell one complete story. One hundred and fifty-six episodes were produced over a year, with Homer Brightman writing a good deal of them.

Brightman's last stint in TV animation was with the studio owned by producer David H. DePatie and by veteran animator/director Isadore "Friz" Freleng. The one series Brightman worked on for them was *The Super 6*, starring six superheroes fighting crime for Super Services, Inc. The show aired on NBC from 1966-69, but it is not known which episodes Brightman scripted.

Brightman's life after Disney also included more work for Disney, yet not in animation. Early in 1957, almost eight years after letting him go, Walt himself called Brightman at home "and asked him to help develop two live-action features."[28] The first one was *Four Fabulous Characters*, which aired on ABC on September 18, 1957, as part of the *Disneyland* TV show. It was actually a mix of existing animated sequences starring the four (actually five) titular characters—Casey Jones (*The Brave Engineer*, 1950), Henry Martin and Grace Coy ("The Martins and the Coys", from *Make Mine Music*, 1946), Mighty Casey ("Casey at the Bat", from *Make Mine Music*, 1946), and John Chapman ("Johnny Appleseed", from *Melody Time*, 1948)—with the live-action narration of Jerry Colonna. Brightman, who had contributed to "Casey at the Bat" with Eric Gurney, probably wrote some of the additional dialogue to tie the four sequences together.

Originally released theatrically as a special cartoon featurette on August 28, 1957, *The Truth About Mother Goose* first aired on TV as part of *Walt Disney's Wonderful World of Color* on November 17, 1963. Hosted by Walt Disney, the program featured original animated sequences featuring Professor Ludwig Von Drake and his assistant, Herman. Von Drake (voiced by Paul Frees) tells the stories behind Mother Goose rhymes, then comments on "Mickey and the Beanstalk" (from *Fun and Fancy Free*, 1947). Walt Disney then closes the show, previewing the following week's episode. Brightman had written "Mickey and the Beanstalk" along with Harry Reeves, Ted Sears, Eldon Dedini, Jack Hannah, and Frank Tashlin, whereas he had not been involved with the story of *The Truth About Mother Goose* (written by Bil Peet). So he was probably hired to provide Walt Disney's introductory and closing lines, while the dialogue for Ludwig Von Drake was written by Joe Rinaldi.

The first actual live-action feature Brightman adapted for TV was *The Ballad of Hector the Stowaway Dog*, based on the book *Hector, the Stowaway Dog* by Kenneth Dodson. It told the story of a travel-loving trained Airedale and it was first released in two episodes, respectively entitled *Where the Heck Is Hector?* and *Who the Heck Is Hector?*, on January 5 and 12, 1964, airing on NBC TV as part of *Walt Disney's Wonderful World of Color*. It was released theatrically overseas in 1967 as *The Million Dollar Collar*.[29]

In 1965, while Walt was still alive, Brightman worked on the theatrical feature *That Darn Cat!*[30]

Concluding Brightman's second stint as a sometime Disney storyman was another live-action feature, *Pablo and the Dancing Chihuahua*. It was about a Mexican boy who finds adventure in the desert while searching for his missing uncle. Joined by a lost Chihuahua dog, the boy then sneaks across the border between Mexico and the USA, and is offered a place to live by the dog's owner, an American tourist. It first aired in two episodes on January 28 and February 4, 1968, as part of *Walt Disney's Wonderful World of Color*. This project had actually been started by Walt Disney before he died on December 15, 1966, so it is likely that Brightman's script had also been prepared in 1966, and later adapted by Paul Lucey (teleplay) and Jack Speirs (narration).[31]

Homer Brightman retired in the 1970s and died of pneumonia in 1988 in Albuquerque, New Mexico, at age eighty-seven.

• •

Alberto Becattini is a Disney historian specializing in the history of Disney comics. From the 1970s onward, he has written hundreds of articles and essays, and since 1992 he has been contributing to Disney magazines published by The Walt Disney Company Italy, writing articles and translating stories. His most famous books are *Disney's Comics, la Storia, i Personaggi: 1930-1995* (Comic Art, 1995), *Floyd Gottfredson* (Comic Art, 1998), and *I Disney Italiani* (Nicola Pesce Editore, 2012) co-authored with Luca Boschi, Leonardo Gori, and Andrea Sani He is a frequent contributor to the *Walt's People* book series.

Homer Brightman: Filmography and Comicography

by Alberto Becattini

Studio: Disney

Animator (15 May 1935–Sept 1935)
Writer/Story Sketch (Sept 1935–1950)

- 14 Dec 1935 *Broken Toys* [Silly Symphony]
- 28 Oct 1936 *Alpine Climbers* [Mickey Mouse]
- 15 Oct 1937 *Clock Cleaners* [Mickey Mouse]
- 21 Dec 1937 *Snow White and the Seven Dwarfs* [Story development, 1935-36]
- 15 Apr 1938 *Donald's Nephews* [Donald Duck]
- 11 May 1938 *Donald's Better Self* [Donald Duck]
- 08 July 1938 *Good Scouts* [Donald Duck]
- 29 July 1938 *The Fox Hunt* [Donald Duck]
- 19 Aug 1938 *The Whalers* [Mickey Mouse]
- 04 Nov 1938 *Donald's Golf Game* [Donald Duck]
- 13 Jan 1939 *Donald's Lucky Day* [Donald Duck]
- 24 Feb 1939 *The Practical Pig* [Special: *The Three little Pigs*]
- 09 June 1939 *Beach Picnic* [Donald Duck]
- 11 Aug 1939 *Donald's Penguin* [Donald Duck]

- 01 Sept 1939 *The Autograph Hound* [Donald Duck]
- 07 Feb 1940 *Pinocchio* [Early story development c.1935]
- 07 June 1940 *Mr. Duck Steps Out* [Donald Duck]
- 13 Dec 1940 *Fire Chief* [Donald Duck]
- 16 Jan 1941 *The Village Smithy* [Donald Duck]
- 07 Mar 1941 *Golden Eggs* [Donald Duck]
- 11 July 1941 *Early to Bed* [Donald Duck]
- 01 Aug 1941 *Truant Officer Donald* [Donald Duck]
- 12 Sept 1941 *Old MacDonald Duck* [Donald Duck]
- 03 Oct 1941 *Lend a Paw* [Pluto]
- 15 Jan 1942 *Donald's Snow Fight* [Donald Duck]
- 01 May 1942 *Donald Gets Drafted* [Donald Duck]
- 24 July 1942 *Donald's Gold Mine* [Donald Duck]
- 25 Sept 1942 *The Vanishing Private* [Donald Duck]
- 18 Dec 1942 *Bellboy Donald* [Donald Duck]
- 29 Jan 1943 *Donald's Tire Trouble* [Donald Duck]
- 06 Feb 1943 *Saludos Amigos* [Sequence: "Lake Titicaca"]
- 19 Feb 1943 *Pluto and the Armadillo* [Mickey Mouse]
- 22 Sept 1944 *First Aiders* [Pluto]
- 26 Jan 1945 *The Clock Watcher* [Donald Duck]
- 03 Feb 1945 *The Three Caballeros* [Sequence: "The Cold-Blooded Penguin"]
- 12 Apr 1945 *Pluto's Kid Brother* [Donald Duck]
- 27 July 1945 *Canine Casanova* [Pluto]
- 09 Oct 1945 *In Dutch* [Pluto]
- 07 Dec 1945 *Canine Patrol* [Pluto]
- 21 Dec 1945 *Old Sequoia* [Donald Duck]
- 12 Apr 1946 *Pluto's Kid Brother* [Pluto]
- 20 Apr 1946 *Make Mine Music* [Sequence: "Casey at the Bat"]
- 20 Sept 1946 *Lighthouse Keeping* [Donald Duck]
- 10 May 1946 *In Dutch* [Pluto]
- 07 June 1946 *Squatter's Rights* [Mickey Mouse]

- 19 July 1946 *The Purloined Pup* [Pluto]
- 30 Aug 1946 *Dumbell of the Yukon* aka *Dumb Bell of the Yukon* [Donald Duck]
- 20 Sept 1946 *Lighthouse Keeping* [Donald Duck]
- 27 Sept 1947 *Fun and Fancy Free* [Sequence: "Mickey and the Beanstalk"]
- 27 May 1948 *Melody Time*
- 05 Oct 1949 *The Adventures of Ichabod and Mr. Toad* [Sequences: "The Wind in the Willows", "Ichabod"]
- 16 Dec 1949 *Toy Tinkers* [Donald Duck]
- 04 Mar 1950 *Cinderella*
- 28 July 1951 *Alice in Wonderland* [Early story development]
- 05 Feb 1953 *Peter Pan* [Early story development]
- 18 Sept 1957 "Four Fabulous Characters" [*Disneyland* TV show, additional dialogue; re-released on 13 Aug 1958, 03 Mar 1964]
- 17 Nov 1963 "The Truth About Mother Goose" [*The Wonderful World of Color* TV show, additional dialogue; re-released on 12 July 1964, 25 Dec 1966, 22 Dec 1974]
- 05–12 Jan 1964 "The Ballad of Hector the Stowaway Dog" [*The Wonderful World of Color* TV show; re-released on 19–26 July 1964, 25 Apr and 2 May 1971]
- 02 Dec 1965 *That Darn Cat!*
- 28 Jan 1968–04 Feb 1968 "Pablo and the Dancing Chihuahua" [*The Wonderful World of Color* TV show; re-released on 23 June 1968, 20 Aug 1972]

Brightman also worked on story development on unproduced shorts which include:

- c.1936–1937 *The Three Bears*
- c.1941 *Morgan's Ghost* [with Harry Reeves and Roy Williams over 1939 typescript by Dick Creedon and Al Perkins]
- c.1945 "The Laughing Gauchito" [proposed sequel to "The Flying Gauchito" sequence in *The Three Caballeros*]
- c.1949 *Seven Mickey Mice*

Studio: Walter Lantz
Writer

- 20 Oct 1952 *The Great Who-Dood-It* aka *The Great Magician* [Woody Woodpecker]
- 20 Apr 1953 *Buccaneer Woodpecker* [Woody Woodpecker]
- 15 June 1953 *Operation Sawdust* [Woody Woodpecker]
- 10 Aug 1953 *Maw and Paw* [Maw and Paw]
- 14 Sept 1953 *Belle Boys* [Woody Woodpecker]
- 26 Sept 1953 *Hypnotic Hick* [Woody Woodpecker]
- 28 Sept 1953 *Plywood Panic* [Maw and Paw]
- 12 Oct 1953 *Hot Noon* or *12 O'Clock for Sure* [Woody Woodpecker]
- 21 Dec 1953 *Chilly Willy* [Chilly Willy]
- 18 Jan 1954 *Socko in Morocco* [Woody Woodpecker]
- 15 Mar 1954 *Alley to Bali* aka *Bali Ho* [Woody Woodpecker]
- 10 May 1954 *Under the Counter Spy* aka *Secret Agent F.O.B.* [Woody Woodpecker]
- 05 July 1954 *Hot Rod Huckster* [Woody Woodpecker]
- 01 Aug 1954 *Paw's Night Out* [Maw and Paw; with Michael Maltese]
- 25 Oct 1954 *A Fine Feathered Frenzy* aka *The Last Chase* [Woody Woodpecker]
- 20 Dec 1954 *I'm Cold* aka *Some Like It Not* [Chilly Willy]
- 14 Mar 1955 *Witch Crafty* [Woody Woodpecker]
- 09 May 1955 *Private-Eye Pooch* [Woody Woodpecker]
- 04 July 1955 *Bedtime Bedlam* [Woody Woodpecker]
- 24 Oct 1955 *Hot and Cold Penguin* [Chilly Willy]
- 09 Dec 1955 *The Tree Medic* [Woody Woodpecker]
- 16 Jan 1956 *Pigeon Holed* [Homer Pigeon]
- 09 Apr 1956 *The Ostrich Egg and I* [Maggie and Sam]
- 04 June 1956 *Room and Wrath* [Chilly Willy]
- 02 July 1956 *Woodpecker from Mars* [Woody Woodpecker]

- 30 July 1956 *Hold That Rock* [Chilly Willy; alternate release date 02 July 1956]
- 27 Aug 1956 *The Talking Dog* [Maggie and Sam]
- 24 Sept 1956 *Calling All Cuckoos* [Woody Woodpecker]
- 17 Dec 1956 *Woody Meets Davy Crewcut* [Woody Woodpecker]
- 19 Nov 1956 *Arts and Flowers* [Woody Woodpecker]
- 14 Jan 1957 *Fowled-Up Party* [Maggie and Sam]
- 08 Apr 1957 *Box Car Bandit* [Woody Woodpecker]
- 06 May 1957 *Operation Cold Feet* [Chilly Willy]
- 29 July 1957 *To Catch a Woodpecker* [Woody Woodpecker]
- 30 Aug 1957 *The Big Snooze* [Chilly Willy; alternate release date 21 Oct 1957]
- 04 Nov 1957 *Fodder and Son* [Woody Woodpecker]
- 18 Nov 1957 *Dopey Dick, the Pink Whale* [Woody Woodpecker]
- 02 Dec 1957 *Swiss Miss-Fit* [Chilly Willy]
- 27 Jan 1958 *Misguided Missile* [Woody Woodpecker]
- 24 Feb 1958 *Watch the Birdie* [Woody Woodpecker]
- 24 Mar 1958 *Salmon Yeggs* [Windy & Breezy]
- 19 May 1958 *Polar Pests* [Chilly Willy]
- 16 June 1958 *A Chilly Reception* [Chilly Willy; alternate release date 11 Aug 1968]
- 14 July 1958 *His Better Elf* [Woody Woodpecker]
- 11 Aug 1958 *Everglade Raid* [Woody Woodpecker; alternate release date 14 July 1968]
- 08 Sept 1958 *Tree's a Crowd* [Woody Woodpecker]
- 06 Oct 1958 *Three Ring Fling* [Windy]
- 03 Nov 1958 *Jittery Jester* [Woody Woodpecker]
- 08 Dec 1958 *Little Televillain* [Chilly Willy]
- 05 Jan 1959 *Truant Student* [Windy & Breezy]
- 02 Feb 1959 *Robinson Gruesome* [Chilly Willy]
- 01 Mar 1959 *Tomcat Combat* [Woody Woodpecker]
- 01 Apr 1959 *Yukon Have It* [Chilly Willy]

- 01 Apr 1959 *Log Jammed* [Woody Woodpecker]
- 01 June 1959 *Bee Bopped* [Windy & Breezy]
- 13 July 1959 *The Tee Bird* [Woody Woodpecker]
- 07 Aug 1959 *Romp in a Swamp* [Woody Woodpecker]
- 07 Sept 1959 *Space Mouse* [Hickory, Dickory and Doc]
- 08 Dec 1959 *Mouse Trapped* [Hickory, Dickory and Doc]
- 05 Jan 1960 *Billion Dollar Boner* [Woody Woodpecker]
- 02 Feb 1960 *Witty Kitty* [Hickory, Dickory and Doc]
- 20 Apr 1960 *Ballyhooey* [Woody Woodpecker]
- 16 June 1960 *Bats in the Belfry* [Woody Woodpecker]
- 13 July 1960 *Ozark Lark* [Woody Woodpecker]
- 10 Aug 1960 *Fish Hooked* [Chilly Willy]
- 29 Nov 1960 *Southern Fried Hospitality* [Woody Woodpecker]
- 20 Dec 1960 *Fowled-Up Falcon* [Woody Woodpecker]
- 10 Jan 1961 *Poop-Deck Pirate* [Woody Woodpecker]
- 31 Jan 1961 *Rough & Tumbleweed* [Inspector Willoughby]
- 14 Feb 1961 *Eggnapper* [Fatso the Bear]
- 07 Mar 1961 *The Bird Who Came to Dinner* [Woody Woodpecker]
- 28 Mar 1961 *Gabby's Diner* [Woody Woodpecker]
- 11 Apr 1961 *Papoose on the Loose* [Cartune]
- 25 Apr 1961 *Clash and Carry* [Chilly Willy]
- 16 May 1961 *St. Moritz Blitz* [Chilly Willy]
- 30 May 1961 *Sufferin' Cats* [Woody Woodpecker]
- 04 July 1961 *Franken-Stymied* [Woody Woodpecker]
- 15 Aug 1961 *Mississippi Slow Boat* [Inspector Willoughby]
- 07 Jan 1964 *Dumb Like a Fox* [Woody Woodpecker]
- 01 Mar 1964 *Deep Freeze Squeeze* [Chilly Willy]
- 09 June 1964 *Freeway Fracas* [Woody Woodpecker]
- 07 July 1964 *Skinfolks* [Woody Woodpecker]
- 01 Aug 1964 *Lighthouse-keeping Blues* [Chilly Willy]
- 03 Aug 1964 *Woody's Clip Joint* [Woody Woodpecker]
- 17 Nov 1964 *Roamin' Roman* [Woody Woodpecker]

- 01 June 1965 *Sioux Me* [Woody Woodpecker]
- 01 June 1965 *Pesty Guest* [Chilly Willy]
- 01 Feb 1966 *Snow Place Like Home* [Chilly Willy]
- 01 Mar 1966 *South Pole Pals* [Chilly Willy]
- 01 May 1966 *Teeny Weeny Meany* [Chilly Willy]
- 01 Jan 1967 *Operation Shanghai* [Chilly Willy]
- 01 June 1967 *Chilly Chums* [Chilly Willy; alternate release date 01 June 1968]
- 01 Dec 1967 *Chiller Dillers* [Chilly Willy; alternate release date 01 June 1968]
- 01 Jan 1968 *Woody the Freeloader* [Woody Woodpecker]
- 01 Feb 1968 *Under Sea Dogs* [Chilly Willy]
- 01 Apr 1968 *Highway Hecklers* [Chilly Willy]
- 1969 *Little Skeeter* [Woody Woodpecker]
- 01 May 1969 *Project Reject* [Chilly Willy]
- 1969 *Woody's Knight Mare* [Woody Woodpecker]
- 01 June 1969 *Tumbleweed Greed* [Woody Woodpecker]
- 1969 *Chilly and the Looney Gooney* [Chilly Willy]
- 1969 *Ship a-Hoy Woody* [Woody Woodpecker]
- 01 Sept 1969 *Prehistoric Super Salesman* [Woody Woodpecker]
- 01 Dec 1969 *Sleepy Time Bear* [Chilly Willy]

Studio: MGM
Writer

- 29 Mar 1957 *Give and Tyke* [Spike and Tyke]
- 26 July 1957 *Scat Cats* [Spike and Tyke]
- 06 Dec 1957 *One Droopy Knight* [Droopy]
- 07 Feb 1958 *Sheep Wrecked* [Droopy]
- 04 Apr 1958 *Mutts About Racing* [Droopy]
- 04 July 1958 *A Droopy Leprechaun* [Droopy]
- 01 Aug 1958 *Tot Watchers* [Tom and Jerry]

Studio: Larry Harmon Picture Corporation
Writer

1959–1962 *Bozo: The World's Most Famous Clown* [TV Series; 52 episodes]

- 01. "Fish Tanks Pranks"
- 02. "A Glutton for Mutton"
- 03. "All Mind Gold Mine"
- 04. "Bad News Cruise"
- 05. "Ball Park Lark"
- 06. "Big Boo Boo on a Fast Choo Choo"
- 07. "Big Clown Shake-Down"
- 08. "Big Dealer on a Stearn Wheeler"
- 09. "Big Flop Train Hop"
- 10. "Big Lab Confab"
- 11. "Big Tree Spree"
- 12. "Bozo's Icy Escapade"
- 13. "Broad Sword Discard"
- 14. "Car Thief Grief"
- 15. "Charter Service Nervous"
- 16. "Chicken Burglar Bungler"
- 17. "Dance of the Ants"
- 18. "Eagle's Nest Pest"
- 19. "Fast Pace Sky Chase"
- 20. "Film-Flam for Ali Kablam"
- 21. "Food Pest Jest"
- 22. "Four Flusher Gusher"
- 23. "Freeloader Railroader"
- 24. "Gate Crasher Smasher"
- 25. "Go-Go Pogo-Pogo"
- 26. "Happy-Gas Gasser"
- 27. "High Fly Rug Spy"

- 28. "Hop-Chest Quest"
- 29. "Hurricane Belinda"
- 30. "Lake Resort Sport"
- 31. "Little Naggin' Dragon"
- 32. "Manhunt Stunts"
- 33. "Mill Pond Thrill Chill"
- 34. "Okey Dokey Hokey Pokey"
- 35. "Papoose on the Loose"
- 36. "Pie in the Eye Guy"
- 37. "Piggy Bank Prank"
- 38. "Razzle Dazzle Castle Hassle"
- 39. "Real Gone Leprechaun"
- 40. "Rickety Rackety Rocketeer"
- 41. "Rockey's Snack Attack"
- 42. "Show Biz Whiz"
- 43. "Sidewalk Peddler's Meddler"
- 44. "Ski Lodge Hodge Podge"
- 45. "South of the Border Disorder"
- 46. "Square Shootin' Square"
- 47. "Super Duper Trouble Shooter"
- 48. "Teeny Weeny Meany"
- 49. "Texas Stranger Danger"
- 50. "The Big Cake Bake"
- 51. "Tip Top Bell Hop"
- 52. "Whipper Snapper Snipper"

110 Life in the Mouse House

Studio: UPA
Writer

Sept 1961–1962 *The Dick Tracy Show* [TV Series; 26 episodes]

- 01. "Pearl Thief Grief"
- 02. "Scrambled Yeggs"
- 03. "Two Heels on Wheels"
- 04. "Mole in the Hole"
- 05. "Champ Chumps"
- 06. "Red Hot Riding Hoods"
- 07. "Surprised Package"
- 08. "Gruesome Twosome"
- 09. "Funny Money"
- 10. "Tick Tock Shock"
- 11. "Bowling Ball Bandits"
- 12. "Horse Race Chase"
- 13. "Kidnap Trap"
- 14. "Rock-a-Bye Guys"
- 15. "The Alligator Baggers"
- 16. "The Boomerang Ring"
- 17. "The Hot Ice Bag"
- 18. "Evil Eye Guy"
- 19. "Fowl Play"
- 20. "The Loch Mess Monster"
- 21. "Lumber Scamps"
- 22. "Ham on the Lam"
- 23. "The Big Seal Steal"
- 24. "The Bird Brain Pickers"
- 25. "The Lie Detector"
- 26. "The Tower of Pizza"

Studio: Cambria

Writer

- 20 Dec 1965–1966 *The New 3 Stooges* [TV Series; unknown episodes]

Studio: De Patie–Freleng

Writer

- 10 Sept 1966–31 Aug 1969 *The Super 6* [TV Series; unknown episodes]

Newspaper Comic Strips

Publisher: Walt Disney Productions, Inc./King Features Syndicate, Inc.

Reportedly, Brightman wrote most of the first two months' releases of the Donald Duck daily strip drawn by Al Taliaferro, between February 7, 1938, and April 6, 1938.

Comic Books

Publisher: Dell/Western Printing/KK Publications, Inc.

- "Donald Duck Finds Pirate Gold" [*Four Color* #9, Sept 1942]. Bob Karp adapted the original screenplay by Harry Reeves, Homer Brightman, and Roy Williams for the unproduced short, *Morgan's Ghost*. Drawn by Carl Barks and Jack Hannah.
- "Mickey Mouse and the Disappearing Island" [*Wheaties Premiums* #A-1, 1950]. Drawn by Don R. Christensen.
- "Zorro: Ghostly Confession" [*Walt Disney's Comics and Stories* #275, Aug 1963]. Drawn by Nat Edson.
- "Zorro: The Golden Pendant" [*Walt Disney's Comics and Stories* #276, Sept 1963]. Drawn by Nat Edson.
- "Zorro: Turnabout" [*Walt Disney's Comics and Stories* #277, Oct 1963]. Drawn by Nat Edson.
- "Zorro: Masquerade Justice" [*Walt Disney's Comics and Stories* #278, Nov 1963]. Drawn by Nat Edson.

Publisher: Walt Disney Productions, Inc.

The following stories were produced by the Western Publishing and the Disney Studio for overseas consumption, within the so-called Studio Program. Stories are listed by code number, i.e., as they were delivered by Brightman. They were not published in this order. The list is partial, as only a few credits are known.

- *Fight with El Cuchillo* [Zorro; S 62004, 1962]. Drawn by Richard Moore.
- Zorro: *Garcia's Masquerade* [Zorro; S 65013, 1965]. Drawn by Dan Spiegle.
- *Smith, the Jeweler* [Huey, Dewey, and Louie; S 65014, 1965]. Drawn by Jim Fletcher and Ellis Eringer.
- *Garcia Does His Duty* [Zorro; S 65046, 1965]. Drawn by Richard Moore.
- *Garcia Gets His Man* [Zorro; S 65073, 1965]. Drawn by Jesse Marsh.
- *The Big Rescue Operation* [Uncle Scrooge; S 65074, 1965]. Drawn by Kay Wright and Ellis Eringer.
- *The Gold Strike* [Zorro; S 65087, 1965]. Drawn by Richard Moore.
- *Red Headed Ape* [Uncle Scrooge; S 65107, 1965]. Drawn by Jim Fletcher and Ellis Eringer.
- *The House on Needlenose Point* [Uncle Scrooge; S 65124, 1965]. Drawn by Jim Fletcher and Ellis Eringer.
- *The Great Yacht Race* [Uncle Scrooge; S 65156, 1965]. Drawn by Jim Fletcher and Ellis Eringer.
- *Counterfeit Zorro* [Zorro; S 65167, 1965]. Drawn by Richard Moore.
- *Zorro and the Protectors* [Zorro; S 65168, 1965]. Drawn by Richard Moore.
- *A Race with Death* [Zorro; S 65169, 1965]. Drawn by Richard Moore.
- *Garcia's Funny Uncle* [Zorro; S 65174, 1965]. Drawn by Mel Keefer

- *Zorro and the Lady Bandit* [Zorro; S 66026, 1966]. Drawn by Richard Moore and Mike Royer.
- *The Swimming Sergeant* [Zorro; S 66073, 1966]. Drawn by Mel Keefer.
- *The Quarantine* [Zorro; S 66077, 1966]. Drawn by Mel Keefer.
- *Hopeless Luck* [Uncle Scrooge; S 66132, 1965]. Drawn by Jack Bradbury and Ellis Eringer.
- *Zorro and the Bull Baiting* [Zorro; S 66155, 1966]. Drawn by Richard Moore.
- *The Indian Raiders* [Zorro; S 66161, 1966]. Drawn by Richard Moore and Mike Royer.
- *The Spanish Cigars* [Zorro; S 67054, 1967]. Drawn by Richard Moore.
- *Zorro and the Abandoned Pet* [Zorro; S 67074, 1967]. Drawn by Richard Moore.
- *Garcia's Lady Love* [Zorro; S 67096, 1967]. Drawn by Richard Moore.
- *The Republica Del Sol* [Zorro; S 69007, 1969]. Drawn by Richard Moore.
- *Garcia's Exercise* [Zorro; S 69015, 1969]. Drawn by Doug Wildey and Richard Moore.
- *Zorro And The Grizzly* [Zorro; S 69058, 1969]. Drawn by Richard Moore.
- *Zorro And The Playful Kinkajou* [Zorro; S 70142S 70006, 1970]. Drawn by Richard Moore.
- *Wall Of Water* [Zorro; S 70142, 1970]. Drawn by Dan Spiegle.

Children's Books
Publisher: Whitman Publishing Company (aka Western Publishing Company)

- *Goofy and His Wonderful Cornet* [Tell-a-Tale #2516, 1964]. Drawn by Pete Alvarado and William Lorencz.
- *Mary Poppins: She's Supercalifragilisticexpialidocius* [Tell-a-Tale #2442/2606, 1964]. Drawn by Jan Neely.
- *Mary Poppins: She's Supercalifragilisticexpialidocius* [Top-Top Tales #2450, 1964]. Drawn by Jan Neely.
- *Uncle Scrooge: Rainbow Runaway* [Big Tell-a-Tale #2422, 1965]. Art by Frank McSavage and Tony Strobl.

Records
Publisher: Decca

- *Woody Woodpecker's Family Album* [#DL 8659, 1957]. Dialogue and stories. Re-released in 1963.

Notes

1 This story is confirmed in an interview of Homer Brightman released in Lori Varosh, "He Gave Disney Ideas", in *Journal American*. Date unknown.

2 WED Enterprises became Walt Disney Imagineering in 1986.

3 In reality, Walt and Roy's trip to Europe took place in June and July 1935. For a detailed account of the trip, see Didier Ghez, *Disney's Grand Tour* (Theme Park Press, 2013).

4 For more information about "Dogstone" (Perce Pearce), see Didier Ghez, "Piercing the Perce Pearce Mystery", in *Walt's People: Volume 12* (Xlibris, 2012).

5 According to John Canemaker, Homer Brightman was hired on March 15, 1935.

6 *Broken Toys* (1935).

7 Works Progress Administration, a New Deal agency that hired unemployed people to carry out public works projects

8 For more information about the genesis of the Donald Duck strip, see Jim Korkis, "Just Ducky: Al Taliaferro and Donald Duck", at http://www.mouseplanet.com/8195/Just_Ducky__Al_Taliaferro_and_Donald_Duck

9 The artist that Homer trained was Bob Karp.

10 Disney historian Alberto Becattini notes: "Arthur Edward (Ted) Thwaites ("Gloomy Gus") actually left Disney on November 9, 1940, and passed away a week later. So I don't really know if he had left Disney for greener fields or because he was ill. He was 54 when he died."

11 *Fortune* magazine, Volume 10, Number 5, November 1934.

12 To learn more about that visit to the Studio by H.G. Wells

and Charlie Chaplin, see Didier Ghez, *Disney's Grand Tour* (Theme Park Press, 2013).

13 For a detailed account of Walt's Field Day, see "Walt's Field Day—1938" by Todd James Pierce at http://www.disneyhistoryinstitute.com/2013/09/walts-field-day-1938.html

14 J.R. Bray and Earl Hurd ("Jiggins") had developed and patented the processes involved in "cel animation".

15 Between March and June 1936, Don Graham, George Drake ("Dogstone"), and Carter Ludlow set up a special office in New York in the RKO Building in Rockefeller Center to recruit new artists for the studio during production of *Snow White*.

16 In his interview with Michael Barrier on May 29, 1971, Frank Tashlin ("Bigger") remembered things differently: "They had had a story for years that they couldn't lick—*Jack and the Beanstalk*—and [Walt] gave that to me. I licked it, I found the raison d'être for that story. But he would never give me credit, and that's where I got into the fight with him. I had broken the back of it and made it work, and he took it away from me and gave it to a couple of his—the whole feeling was, how can this guy, who's come from another studio, solve this problem that we haven't been able to solve? They took it away, and they made some changes, but they didn't change the basic story. That was our argument, and I left.

"That was my story. I came up with the idea that made it work, which was that when this harp was played, it gave prosperity to the land, and it had been stolen. Another thing I laid out on the Leica reel—I laid it out for Wilfred Jackson, who was a great director—was called the "beanero", and that was [the beanstalk] growing at night. We had a whole piece of music that Oliver Wallace wrote for the beanstalk growing and lifting up the house. When we did that on the Leica reel, I tell you it was just marvelous. There it all was, the music and everything. I never saw it in the film—I always had a kind of heartache about that." See Didier Ghez (editor), *Walt's People: Volume 2* (Xlibris, 2005).

17 Walt and "El Grupo" left for Latin America on August 11, 1941.

18 Art Babbitt.

19 Florencio Molina Campos.

20 Riley Allen Thomson Sr.

21 Raymond Forrest Farwell.

22 In reality, according to J.B. Kaufman, author of *South of the Border with Disney: Walt Disney and the Good Neighbor Program 1941-1948* (Disney Editions, 2009), the party went in three groups. Brightman was in the first one, leaving on December 8, along with Norm Ferguson, Jack Cutting, and Edmundo Santos. The second group left on December 9: Walt and Lillian Disney, Mary Blair, Ken Anderson, Eric Larson, and Fred Moore. The third group departed on December 10: Chuck Wolcott and Ernie Terrazas. They seem to have all returned together on December 23.

In March and April 1943, there was a second trip. Sam Slyfield and his wife went first on March 18. The second party, Wolcott, Santos, and Dunham, followed on March 20. Finally, Brightman and Terrazas went down on the 24th, but they stayed together and went on side trips. The last group left on the 28th: Walt and Lillian, Ferguson, and Dorothy Hughes. Ferguson, Brightman, and Terrazas returned to Los Angeles on April 7.

23 Art historian Magdalena Acosta Urquidi wrote: "Two of the most interesting, yet unknown amateur filmmakers of the thirties are Harry Wright and his younger brother, Samuel Bolling. The Wrights were born in Bedford, Virginia, toward the end of the 19th century. When their father died, Harry, the eldest, got a job as a traveling buyer of scrap metal for the Joseph Iron and Equipment Co., and was sent by the company to Mexico in 1900. He was so successful that he asked his brother Bolling to join him in 1902. Five years later, they started their own foundry, the famous "La Consolidada S.A." (Consolidated Iron and Equipment Co.), making both of them millionaires during the early part of the 20th century.

[...]

"Harry was gregarious and had a real passion for travel and cinematography. As a millionaire and golf fan, he naturally joined the exclusive Circumnavigators Club, and, according to his own testimony, traveled around the globe five times and "visited every country in the world". Later on, he became a member of the Amateur Cinema League and founding member and president of the Cinema Club de México, in 1937.

"The Kraal Theatre, built on the grounds of Harry Wright's residence in downtown Mexico City, became the favorite meeting place for amateur filmmakers. It had approximately forty members, including prominent politicians, businessmen, and members of the expatriate community.

[...]

"Both of the Wright brothers had movie theaters at home, but *Movie Makers* magazine described Harry's Kraal Theatre as 'the most interesting private theatre in Mexico and one of the finest in the world (...)'. An important feature of the Kraal was Harry Wright's collection of more than 2,000 films, including many of his own shot in the Soviet Union, North Africa, Mexico, the Middle East, and Europe, which he showed regularly to his immediate social circle, and occasionally to foreign celebrities visiting the country."

See Magdalena Acosta Urquidi, *The Amateur Films of the Wright Brothers*, in the catalog of the 8th International Film Festival of Morelia (October 16-24, 2010).

In 1939, Harry Wright had contacted Disney's representative in Mexico, Robert Hartmann, to lease some 16mm Disney movies for his private theatre. Roy O. Disney had accepted the request in a letter to Robert Hartmann dated August 24, 1939.

24 Lou Clayton was Durante's long-time manager.

25 Homer Brightman's personnel card no longer exists at the Walt Disney Archives, and the exact date at which he left the Studio is unclear, but he quotes 1950 in an interview he granted to journalist Rick Nathanson of the *Albuquerque Journal* at the end of his life.

26 Alberto Becattini, unpublished interview with Mary Jim Karp, 1984.

27 Alberto Becattini, "Jack Bradbury: An Interview with a Funny Animal Maestro" in *Comic Book Marketplace* no. 103, June 2003. p. 61.

28 John Canemaker, *Paper Dreams* (Hyperion, 1999).

29 Bill Cotter, *The Wonderful World of Disney Television, A Complete History* (unpublished unedited manuscript).

30 Lori Varosh, "He Gave Disney Ideas" in *Journal American*. Date unknown.

31 Bill Cotter, *The Wonderful World of Disney Television, A Complete History* (unpublished unedited manuscript).

About the Author

Homer Brightman was one of the members of Disney's Story Department from 1935 to 1950, right in the middle of the Golden Age of Disney animation.

During those fifteen years, he was often teamed with another legendary story artist, Harry Reeves, and was instrumental in developing dozens of storyboards for some of the most famous Disney shorts, many of them featuring Donald and Pluto. Among the classic shorts tackled by Brightman: *Alpine Climbers, The Fox Hunt, Clock Cleaners, Beach Picnic, The Fire Chief,* and *Lend a Paw.*

Homer also worked on several of the features, including *Snow White, Pinocchio, Bambi, Saludos Amigos, The Three Caballeros, Make Mine Music, Fun and Fancy Free, Melody Time, The Adventures of Ichabod and Mr. Toad,* and *Cinderella.*

As part of the Story Department, Homer was at the very heart of the Disney Studio, and worked with some of its stars, including Ted Sears, Dave Hand, Perce Pearce, Roy Williams, Carl Barks, Ham Luske, and Frenchy de Trémaudan.

After Disney, Brightman joined UPA, MGM, and Walter Lantz. He passed away in 1988.

About the Editor

Didier Ghez has conducted Disney research since he was a teenager in the mid '80s. His articles about the parks, animation, and vintage international Disneyana, as well as' his many interviews with Disney artists, have appeared in such magazines as *Disney Twenty-Three, Persistence of Vision, Tomart's Disneyana Update, Animation Journal, Animation Magazine, StoryboarD,* and *Fantasyline.* He is the author of the book *Disney's Grand Tour,* co-author of the art book *Disneyland Paris—From Sketch to Reality,* and co-editor of *Inside the Whimsy Works: My Life with Walt Disney Productions.* He runs The Disney History blog (disneybooks.blogspot.com), The Disney Books Network website (www.pizarro.net/didier), and serves as managing editor of the *Walt's People* book series.

About the Publisher

Theme Park Press is the largest independent publisher of Disney and Disney-related books in the world.

Established in November 2012 by Bob McLain, Theme Park Press has expanded quickly, with over two dozen books scheduled for release in 2014, ranging from park guidebooks and fiction to historical monographs, biographies, and in-depth treatments of theme park rides and attractions.

For more information, please visit:

http://themeparkpress.com

Index

Adventures of Dick Tracy, The 98

Alice in Cartoonland 11

Alpine Climbers 12, 14, 101, 119

Animation Director (Jack Kinney) xxi, 59

Apalini (Bianca Majolie) xxi, 35

Argentine Artist (F. Molina Campos) xxi, 69

Ballad of Hector the Stowaway Dog, The 99, 103

Bambi 45, 49-50, 84, 119

Band Concert, The 33

Barbera, Joe 97

Barker (Pinto Colving) xxi, 17

Bell Boy Donald 57

Belter (Jack Hannah) xxi, 51-52

Bergen, Edgar 85

Bigger (Frank Tashlin) xxi, 55, 116

Boney Australian (Ken O'Connor) xxi, 4

Bozo the Clown 98

Bradbury, Jack 95, 113, 118

Brown, Dick 98

Cambria Animation Studios 98

Cartune 98, 106

Casey at the Bat 84-85, 99, 102

Chaplin, Charlie 32, 116

Chief Agitator (Art Babbitt) xxi, 67

Chilby (Eddie Strickland) xxi, 4-5

Chilly Willy 96-97, 104-107

Cinderella xii, 11, 88-92, 103, 119

Clem Longshanks (Carl Barks) xxi, 13, 18, 96, 111, 119

Clock Cleaners 28, 101, 119

Colonna, Jerry 99

Crock (Card Walker) xxi, 91

Davis, Jim 95

Decca 97, 114

DePatie, David 98

Dick Tracy Show, The 98, 110

Diddle (Joe Grant) xxi, 13, 15, 17

Dill (Ernie Terrazas) xxi, 38-39, 66, 71, 75

Disneyland TV show 99, 103

Dodger (Norman Ferguson) xxi, 80-81

Dogstone (George Drake) xxi, 3-5, 42, 48, 115-116

Donald Duck xii, xiii, 11-12, 14, 19, 27-28, 38, 50-52, 57, 68, 80, 95, 101-103, 111, 115, 119

Donald's Show Fight 57

Duddleham (Otto Englander) xxi, 28, 37-38

Durante, Jimmy 84

Edson, Nat 96, 111

Fire Chief, The 50, 52, 102, 119

Fluk (Probably Carl Fallberg) xxi, 28

Former Polo Player (James Bodrero) xxi, 64

Fortune 25, 115

Four Fabulous Characters 99, 103

Fox Hunt, The 27, 101, 119
Freleng, Friz 98
Fun and Fancy Free 83, 85, 99, 103, 119
Gabbey (Tom Wood) xxi, 8
Gilbert, Billy 85
Gillette, Edwin 98
Gloomy Gus (Ted Thwaites) xxi, 19, 115
Good Housekeeping 8, 19
Goofy xiii, 27-28, 59-60, 67-69, 96, 114
Grout (Dick Lundy) xxi, 19
Haas, Clark 98
Hanna, Bill 97
Harding, Laverne 97
Henry (unidentified) xxi, 2
Hispanic Animator (Rudy Zamora) xxi, 33
Hogsworth (Roy Scott) xxi, 6-8, 11, 18-19
How to Be a Sailor 60, 67-68
Hubbard, Al 95
Hultgren, Ken 95
Ichabod and Mr. Toad 83, 103, 119
Inspector Willoughby 97, 106
Ivy Green (Mary Flanigan) xxi, 2
Jack and the Beanstalk 55, 57, 85, 116
Jacobs, Raymond 97
Jiggins (Earl Hurd) xxi, 46-47, 116
Karp, Bob 95, 111, 115
Karp, Hubie 95
Keefer, Mel 96, 112-113
Kinch (Ben Sharpsteen) xxi, 89-90

Kipper (Wilfred Jackson) xxi, 92
Lantz, Walter 96-98, 104, 119
Lend a Paw 53, 59, 102, 119
Links (Ham Luske) xxi, 20, 92
Loganbary (Josh Meador) xxi, 81-82
Los Angeles Examiner 46-47
Lovy, Alex 96-97
Ludwig von Drake 99
MacPew (McLaren Stewart) xxi, 6-8
Maggie and Sam 96, 104-105
Make Mine Music 83, 85-86, 99, 102, 119
Marsh, Jesse 96, 112
Mary Poppins 96, 114
Maurer, Norman 98
Maw and Paw 96, 104
McCarthy, Charlie 85
Melody Time 83, 99, 103, 119
Mert Kibble (Joe Grant) xxi, 86
Mexico 71-76, 78-80, 100, 117-118
MGM 84, 87-88, 97-98, 107, 119
Mickey Mouse xiii, 11-12, 14-15, 17-19, 27-28, 33, 38, 46, 50, 57, 76, 85, 95, 99, 101-103, 111
Mickey's Birthday Party 57
Midnight and Jeremiah 50
Monks (Frenchy de Trémaudan) xxi, 50-51, 53, 55, 59
Moore, Richard 112-113
Muggle (Ken Anderson) xxi, 69-70
New Three Stooges, The 98
Number Two (Dave Hand) xxi, 50
Orphan's Benefit 19

Pablo and the Dancing Chihuahua 100, 103

Patterson, Don 96

Patton, Luana 85

Peter Pan 88-89, 103

Pinocchio 45, 49, 84-85, 102, 119

Pluto 12-15, 17-18, 38, 53, 102-103, 119

Pophoff (Harry Reeves) xxi, 12, 31-34, 37-38, 42-43, 51-52, 89-90, 92

President Van Buren 21

Rinaldi, Joe 99

Robert Dollar Steamship Lines xv, 21

Rockerduck 96

Rules of the Nautical Road 71

Saludos Amigos 67, 69, 71, 102, 119

Sandifer, Dalton 97

Saperstein, Henry G. 98

Saturday Evening Post xii, 24

Scrooge 96, 112-114

Sligh (Ted Sears) xxi, 9, 11-18, 42-43, 46, 64, 81, 89-90, 92

Smirks (Harry Tytle) xxi, 60, 65

Smith, Paul J. 96-97

Sneezy 86

Snerd, Mortimer 85

Snojob (Perce Pearce) xxi, 4-5, 42-43, 49-50

Snow White and the Seven Dwarfs 11, 47, 101

So Dear to My Heart 50

Sorrell, Herb 60

Spiegle, Dan 96, 112-113

Stiltwalker (Bill Roberts) xxi, 1-3, 5

Strayshott (Webb Smith) xxi, 12-13, 18, 28-29, 37-38, 51, 64

Strike xix, 60-67, 84

Suggs (Roy Williams) xxi, 31-32, 34-37, 48-49

Taliaferro, Al 95, 111, 115

That Darn Cat! 99, 103

Three Caballeros, The 80-81, 85, 96, 102-103, 119

Titcomb (Jack Miller) xxi, 6-8

Tom and Jerry 98, 107

Tricklebank (Frank Teague) xxi, 6-7, 42-43

Truth About Mother Goose, The 99, 103

UPA 98, 110, 119

Walt Disney's Comics and Stories 96, 111

Walt's Disney's Wonderful World of Color 99-100

Walt's Field Day 46

Wells, H.G. 32

Western Printing 95, 111

Wetmore (Hal Adelquist) xxi, 60, 84, 87-90, 92

Williams, Guy 96

Willie the Giant 85

Wise Little Hen, The 19

Woody Woodpecker 96-97, 104-107, 114

Wright, Harry 76-77, 117-118

Wynken, Blynken, and Nod 6

Zaire (Mary Blair) xxi, 68

Zorro 96, 111-113

More Books from Theme Park Press

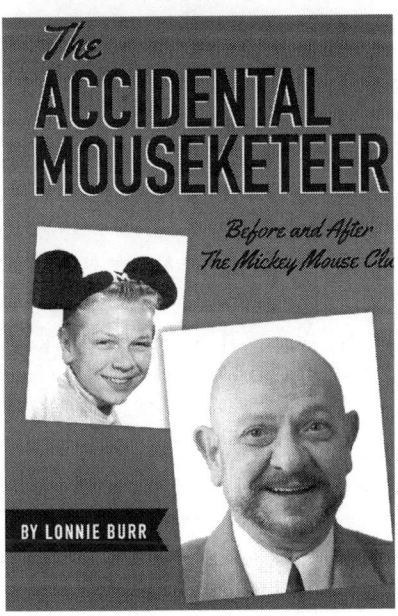

To see all our books, visit ThemeParkPress.com

Made in the USA
Lexington, KY
16 October 2015